Life As We KNOW IT

PLANTS

WATER

REPTILES

CELLS

HABITAT

HERBIVORES

DNA

SHELTER

MAMMALS

HIBERNATION

DK

Penguin Random House

Project Editor Wendy Horobin
Project Art Editors Laura Roberts-Jensen,
Johnny Pau, Amy Orsborne, Poppy Joslin
Editors Paula Regan, Scarlett O'Hara, Sam Atkinson
US Editor Shannon Beatty
Consultant Kim Dennis-Bryan
Production Editor Luca Frassinetti
Production Controller Angela Graef
Managing Editor Esther Ripley
Managing Art Editor Karen Self
Publisher Laura Buller
Associate Publishing Director Liz Wheeler
Art Director Phil Ormerod
Publishing Director Jonathan Metcalf
Jacket Editor Manisha Majithia
Jacket Designer Laura Brim
Jacket Design Development Manager
Sophia MT Turner

REVISED EDITION
Senior editors Fleur Star, Sreshtha Bhattacharya
Senior art editor Spencer Holbrook
US editor Allison Singer
Assistant art editor Nidhi Rastogi
Senior DTP designer Harish Aggarwal
DTP designer Sachin Gupta
Jacket designer Surabhi Wadhwa
Jacket assistant Claire Gell
Jacket design development manager Sophia MTT
Producer, pre-production Gillian Reid
Producer Vivienne Yong
Managing editors Linda Esposito, Kingshuk Ghoshal
Managing art editors Philip Letsu, Govind Mittal
Publisher Andrew Macintyre
Associate publishing director Liz Wheeler
Publishing director Jonathan Metcalf

First American Edition, 2012
This edition published in the United States in 2016 by
DK Publishing, 345 Hudson Street, New York, New York 10014

A catalog record for this book is available
from the Library of Congress.

ISBN 978-1-4654-5138-5

DK books are available at special discounts when purchased
in bulk for sales promotions, premiums, fund-raising,
or educational use. For details, contact:
DK Publishing Special Markets, 345 Hudson Street,
New York, New York 10014

Printed and bound in China

A WORLD OF IDEAS:
SEE ALL THERE IS TO KNOW

www.dk.com

We humans now live **healthier, longer lives** than ever before. It is science, and the study of our world around us, which has made this possible. Although *our planet is well over four billion years old*, our species, *Homo sapiens*, has only existed for a relatively short time. In less than 100,000 years we have *developed the tools* that allow us to ask—and sometimes answer— the big scientific questions. And now we can not only study life, but even start to **create small primitive organisms** in our laboratories.

Perhaps the biggest question is *"What is life?"* It sounds so simple, and yet we still cannot fully answer it. Nor do we know exactly when, how, and where life started or *all the complex questions* about how we, and other creatures, evolved. And of course, we do not know whether there are **forms of life** in other parts of the Universe; perhaps it exists *on some remote planet* that we may never see.

This book explores some of these remarkable questions and *celebrates what we know about our life* and the living creatures and organisms that surround us. It is an **amazing story** and I hope by reading this book you will be as excited about the **study of life**—the science we call biology—as I am.

ROBERT WINSTON

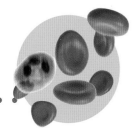

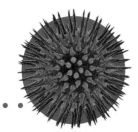

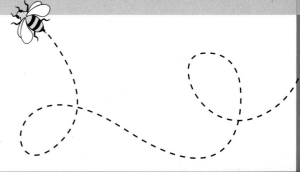

The meaning of LIFE

Scientists and philosophers have been asking "What is life?" for thousands of years. It is one of the hardest questions to answer with certainty, along with the other big question: "How did life begin?" Theories exist but *no one is certain* exactly how and where it began. What we do know is that *Earth is 4.6 billion years old* and simple, single-celled life began 3.5 billion years ago. After that, *life became a lot more complicated!*

What is life?

To ask "**What is life?**" is to ask one of the *trickiest questions* in the Universe. People have been *pondering* **what life is** for *thousands of years,* but **have yet** to come up with a *definite answer*.

ARISTOTLE

The *Greek philosopher* Aristotle was one of the first people to try and pin it down. He thought **life** was anything that *grows, maintains,* and *reproduces* itself. That's certainly true of anything we normally think of as alive—animals, plants, and fungi. But there are many other things that fit this description that we would not usually describe as being alive, such as *fire* or a *computer virus*.

I'm ALIVE— you're just an imposter puppy!

What's the difference between you and me?

Since **Aristotle**, many other people have tried to *define* life, but there is always something **non-living** that manages to *slip through a crack* in every argument.

Perhaps we won't really be able to say what life is until we find it *elsewhere* in the **Universe**. All we have to go on at the moment is our knowledge of what life is like *on our planet.* As far as we know, life exists on Earth and nowhere else. However, the "ingredients" of life have been found in space, and so there may be other life forms out there. Life may look and behave *differently* elsewhere. Ultimately, we may have to change our whole way of *thinking* about **what life is**.

FEATURES OF LIFE

There are certain KEY THINGS that scientists agree define life. For *something to be living* it must:

- Be organized into a shape (for example, a body) with everything inside it working together
- Take in energy and expend it
- Grow, develop, and change
- Reproduce and pass on useful characteristics to its offspring
- Respond to conditions such as light, wind, heat, and water
- Evolve over generations to adapt to its environment.

HOW life

WHERE AND HOW LIFE BEGAN are questions that nobody really knows the answers to. Scientists have a number of theories but Earth has undergone so many changes that there is no longer any firm evidence for exactly how it started. Life could have stopped and started several times before conditions became stable enough for living things to survive.

Toxic planet

Earth formed about 4.6 billion years ago. In the beginning it was a hot, molten rock surrounded by poisonous gases and deadly radiation. Gradually, it cooled and a surface crust formed. Volcanoes spat out gases from the core, filling the atmosphere with carbon dioxide, nitrogen, and water vapor. As the cooling continued, the water vapor turned into liquid and rained down to form the oceans. Although Earth was still a hostile place, it was ready for life to start.

CHEMICAL SOUP

Life probably began in the oceans. All the elements in living things—carbon, hydrogen, nitrogen, oxygen, phosphorus, and sulphur—were present in the atmosphere, but in a different mixture from today. Lightning bolts caused chemical reactions. These formed simple chemicals that washed into the oceans, where they reacted with others to form more complex molecules. Some of these molecules developed an ability to copy themselves. Once they could do that, the development of life speeded up.

GROWING A THICK SKIN

These self-copying molecules were fragile and needed protection from the harsh conditions. One type of molecule, a phospholipid, could form into bubbles, trapping copier molecules inside them. The bubble acted as a barrier, allowing the molecules inside to produce new substances more easily. These were the first cells—the basic units of life.

EARLY CELLS

BEGAN

IT CAME FROM OUTER SPACE

It is possible that some of the chemicals that form the building blocks of life came from elsewhere in the galaxy. In its early days, Earth was under constant bombardment from comets, asteroids, and meteors. Scientists have discovered sugars and amino acids in meteorites. Both of these substances are used to make larger molecules called proteins, which build and maintain cells.

METEOR SHOWER

DEEP SEA VENTS

Perhaps life began around openings in the ocean floor called hydrothermal vents. The heated water spewing out of these vents may have provided the energy for chemical reactions. Bacteria have been found living in these vents, surviving on the sulphurous compounds they emit, without the need for light or oxygen. These conditions are probably similar to those that existed in the early days of Earth.

STROMATOLITES

INDEPENDENT LIFE

The earliest physical evidence we have for the formation of cells comes from fossilized structures called stromatolites. These are around 3.5 billion years old, although scientists think the first cells may have originated 3.8 billion years ago. Stromatolites played a crucial role in oxygenating the atmosphere so life could move onto the land. Stromatolites are still forming today, and are made of mats of cyanobacteria (blue-green algae).

The *building*

All life is based on chemistry. There are 92 natural elements on Earth. These are the substances from which all other things

CAPTAIN CARBON

CRUCIAL CARBON

Carbon is the most important element for life on Earth. It has a unique ability to form molecules of different shapes, especially long chains and hexagonal rings. Molecules that contain carbon are called organic compounds. There are four types of carbon compound that are crucial to all living things: carbohydrates, lipids, proteins, and nucleic acids.

*There's no getting away from me. **I'm totally essential** for all living things!*

In the human body, carbon is the *second most abundant element* after *oxygen*.

Proteins are vital molecules in any organism. They are used for everything from building cells (the simplest living part of an organism) to speeding up reactions and transporting other molecules. Proteins are large, and are made up of smaller units called amino acids. Although there are more than 200 different amino acids, the proteins in most organisms are made from just 20.

Lipids are greasy or waxy substances that include fats and oils. They are made of long chains of carbon and hydrogen atoms. Lipids are needed to form cell membranes (the outer surfaces of cells) and are a useful way to store energy. The human body can make some lipids on its own, but has to get others from the things we eat, such as animal fat, butter, and cooking oil.

Carbohydrates are made of carbon rings with hydrogen and oxygen atoms attached. The simplest types have just one carbon ring and these include sugars, which provide energy. Sugars can be found in many foods, such as honey, fruits, and berries. More complex carbohydrates form long and branching chains of rings and include starch and cellulose, which are found in plants.

Nucleic acids carry the instructions for making proteins and, therefore, all living things. They contain information that controls how a cell functions and reproduces. There are two types: RNA (ribonucleic acid) and DNA (deoxyribonucleic acid). DNA is the most important molecule in the body.

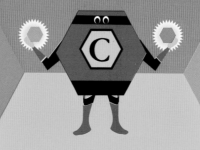

blocks of LIFE

are made. Out of these, 25 are essential for life, and six are used as the building blocks for all living things—carbon, hydrogen, oxygen, nitrogen, sulphur, and phosphorus.

INDISPENSABLE DNA

DNA is found in every cell in our bodies, and carries the information that is needed to make each cell function and reproduce properly. DNA is like an instruction manual that's all in code. It is made up of four chemicals, called nucleotides. These are adenine, cytosine, thymine, and guanine. When making the DNA code, adenine always pairs up with thymine and cytosine pairs with guanine. They are arranged in pairs in spiral chains that look like a twisted ladder, which is known as a double helix.

REPRODUCING ITSELF

Every time a cell needs to reproduce, the DNA unzips along the middle of its "rungs" into two strands. Each of these strands then creates the other side of the "ladder." When the process is finished there is an exact copy of the original DNA chain.

MAKING PROTEINS

DNA is also used to make new proteins for a cell. When a new protein is required, the section of DNA that is the code for that protein unzips and is copied by a molecule called messenger RNA. The messenger RNA moves the copied section to another part of the cell to make the protein.

The human body is made up of hundreds of different carbon compounds.

Thymine

Adenine

Cytosine

Guanine

New strands of DNA

When DNA splits, each strand acts as a template to make the other side of the helix because the nucleotides always pair up with their partner.

down to BASICS

The most BASIC UNIT OF LIFE is the CELL. Every living thing is made up of cells. The simplest is no more than a single cell while a human is made of an estimated *37 trillion* cells (and maybe as many as 724 trillion cells!).

There are *millions* of different types of *cells*.

Each can take in *nutrients to provide itself with energy*, carry out *particular functions*, and replicate itself to form *new cells*.

CELL STRUCTURE
Cells fall into two groups: simple prokaryotes and complex eukaryotes.

Eukaryotes
Eukaryotes are complex cells found in plants, animals, and fungi. They are around 10 times larger than single-celled prokaryotes and contain small compartments called organelles—the cell's equivalent to our body's organs—that carry out the functions of the cell. The most important of these is the nucleus, which houses the cell's DNA.

Cell membrane
Outer boundary of the cell

Mitochondrion
Cell "engine" that turns food into energy

Endoplasmic reticulum
Transports proteins made by the ribosomes around the cell

Nucleolus
Makes ribosomes

Nucleus
Cell's control center

Cytoplasm
Jelly-like substance inside a cell

Lysosomes
Contain digestive enzymes

Golgi complex
Processes, packages, and secretes proteins

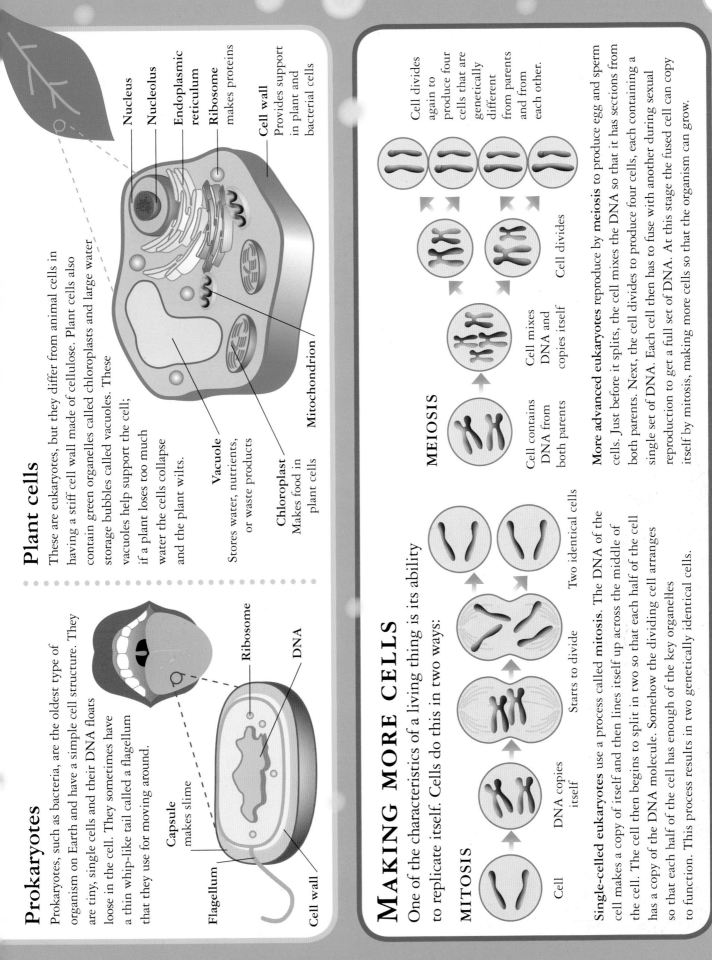

Plant cells

These are eukaryotes, but they differ from animal cells in having a stiff cell wall made of cellulose. Plant cells also contain green organelles called chloroplasts and large water storage bubbles called vacuoles. These vacuoles help support the cell; if a plant loses too much water the cells collapse and the plant wilts.

Nucleus

Nucleolus

Endoplasmic reticulum

Ribosome
makes proteins

Cell wall
Provides support in plant and bacterial cells

Mitochondrion

Vacuole
Stores water, nutrients, or waste products

Chloroplast
Makes food in plant cells

Prokaryotes

Prokaryotes, such as bacteria, are the oldest type of organism on Earth and have a simple cell structure. They are tiny, single cells and their DNA floats loose in the cell. They sometimes have a thin whip-like tail called a flagellum that they use for moving around.

Capsule
makes slime

Flagellum

Cell wall

Ribosome

DNA

MAKING MORE CELLS

One of the characteristics of a living thing is its ability to replicate itself. Cells do this in two ways:

MITOSIS

Cell   DNA copies itself   Starts to divide   Two identical cells

MEIOSIS

Cell contains DNA from both parents   Cell mixes DNA and copies itself   Cell divides   Cell divides again to produce four cells that are genetically different from parents and from each other.

Single-celled eukaryotes use a process called **mitosis**. The DNA of the cell makes a copy of itself and then lines itself up across the middle of the cell. The cell then begins to split in two so that each half of the cell has a copy of the DNA molecule. Somehow the dividing cell arranges so that each half of the cell has enough of the key organelles to function. This process results in two genetically identical cells.

More advanced eukaryotes reproduce by **meiosis** to produce egg and sperm cells. Just before it splits, the cell mixes the DNA so that it has sections from both parents. Next, the cell divides to produce four cells, each containing a single set of DNA. Each cell then has to fuse with another during sexual reproduction to get a full set of DNA. At this stage the fused cell can copy itself by mitosis, making more cells so that the organism can grow.

The factory INSIDE a CELL

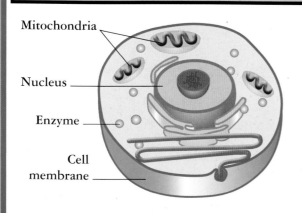

Mitochondria

Nucleus

Enzyme

Cell membrane

Like tiny factories, every cell in your body is a hive of activity. *Thousands of chemical reactions* are taking place there every second, providing you with energy, building your body, and allowing you to breathe, move, and think.

CELL MEMBRANE

FOOD-PROCESSING DEPOT

ENZYMES are the workhorses of a cell. Even a bacterium has around 1,000 different enzymes floating inside it, busily carrying out chemical reactions that split or join molecules together. Enzymes are proteins and each folds up into a unique shape. That shape allows it to carry out one specific reaction and do it quickly and efficiently. Enzymes are named after the chemicals they process. This one is called maltase.

Maltose

Glucose

Maltose for processing

The maltase enzyme splits a sugar called maltose.

The maltose molecule slots into the enzyme, which breaks its central bond.

This makes two molecules of glucose, which are released back into the cell.

One maltase *enzyme* can process *1,000 maltose molecules* a second.

ENERGY DEPOT

One of the most important jobs that enzymes have to do is to make energy for the cell. A team of enzymes carry out a process called glycolysis, which converts glucose into new molecules.

These include two molecules of a chemical called pyruvate and two molecules of an energy-rich compound called adenosine triphosphate (ATP). Some ATP is stored and the rest travels to the mitochondria with the pyruvate.

Pyruvate   ATP

Glucose for processing

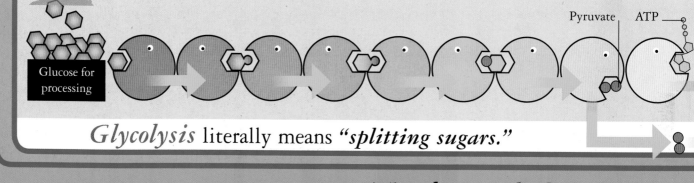

Glycolysis literally means *"splitting sugars."*

The *human body* replaces

CONTROL CENTER

The NUCLEUS is found only in eukaryotic cells. It acts as a control center, sending and receiving messages to and from other cells, and deciding how the cell works. It also controls how the cell grows and replicates itself. The blueprint for the cell, its DNA, is held in the nucleus. The DNA is coiled into strands, called chromosomes. The region of a chromosome that tells the cell how to make a specific protein is called a gene. Human cells contain around 30,000 genes arranged on 46 chromosomes. When the cell needs to make new proteins part of the DNA unzips and copies the right sequence for that protein.

ATP MOLECULE STORE

EXIT TO REST OF CELL

ATP is vital to the working of a cell. It helps move substances in and out of the cell membranes, supplies the energy needed for work, and acts as a switch to control chemical reactions. Its energy is released by splitting off one or more of its phosphate groups. Each cell contains around one billion molecules of ATP, which are constantly being used and recycled.

ATP

Phosphate group

We've split nearly a billion molecules today.

Phosphate groups

CELL MEMBRANE

LIFT TO ATP STORE

TO MITOCHONDRIA

In the mitochondria the molecules undergo a second set of reactions called the citric acid cycle that turn the pyruvate into carbon dioxide and water and create more molecules of ATP.

ATP for storing

ATP

Pyruvate for processing

SPECIAL CELLS

The human body contains around 200 different types of cells. Some group together to form the tissues that make up the body's organs, such as the brain, heart, skin, and lungs. Within these tissues are highly specialist cells that do a particular job. There are blood cells, hair cells, fat cells, bone cells, pigment cells, and eye cells that help you see in color and black and white.

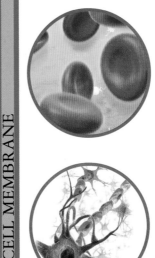

BLOOD CELLS are used to carry oxygen around the body and collect carbon dioxide. They are replaced every 120 days.

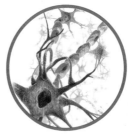

NEURONS are nerve cells that transmit signals to and from all parts of the body. Some can be several feet in length.

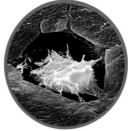

BONE CELLS are made in the marrow of the large bones. As they develop and grow they harden to give the bone strength.

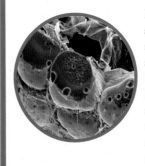

FAT CELLS are used to store energy and insulate the body against heat loss. They are mainly found under the skin and around the major organs.

1 billion cells every hour.

Green ENERGY

Like animals, plants need food to **grow** and **survive**. Unlike animals, they can't move around to find it—instead they have to make food themselves. They do this using a process called *photosynthesis*. All they need is CARBON DIOXIDE, WATER, and SUNLIGHT.

LIVING ON SUNSHINE

The Sun is the source of the energy that all organisms need to live. It arrives on Earth as sunlight, although only a tiny fraction is absorbed by plants. They use that energy to power a series of chemical reactions in their leaves that make energy-rich compounds called sugars, which can be stored by the plant. When sugars are broken down in the cell they release their energy so that the cell can carry out vital functions. Green algae and some bacteria photosynthesize, too.

Power cells

The reaction that converts light into food happens inside the leaves of plants. The membranes that surround leaf cells are full of tiny structures called chloroplasts. These are where the photosynthesis reaction takes place. Chloroplasts are full of a green pigment called chlorophyll. This is what gives plants their green color.

CHLOROPLASTS

Inside the leaf

Air is drawn into the leaf through tiny openings on its underside called stomata (a single one is called a stoma). Air contains only 0.04 percent carbon dioxide, but this is enough for plants to make food. The water needed for photosynthesis to take place is drawn up from the plant's roots and carried through the stem to the leaf cells.

TOP OF LEAF

STOMA

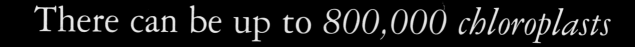

There can be up to *800,000 chloroplasts*

CHLOROPHYLL

Chlorophyll is a vital molecule because it captures sunlight. It is not the only pigment found in plants, but it is the most common. The other pigments absorb different colors of light than chlorophyll but can still be used for photosynthesis.

Changing colors

In the fall, the days shorten and there is less light for photosynthesis. Some trees and shrubs prepare for this by losing their leaves. The chlorophyll starts to break down, revealing the yellow and orange pigments that are also in the leaf. Any sugar that is trapped in the leaf is used to make red, purple, and crimson pigments.

In the fall, leaves change colors.

MELVIN CALVIN

This is how plants make energy:

Carbon dioxide + water + light = glucose + oxygen

This process is called

PHOTOSYNTHESIS.

American scientist **Melvin Calvin** discovered how the dark reaction in photosynthesis works—in 1961 he won the Nobel prize for chemistry.

LIGHT...

Photosynthesis is carried out in two stages: the light and dark reactions. In the light reaction, the sunlight is captured by the chlorophyll and its energy is used to make ATP, a molecule that transports energy around the cell (see pp.16–17). During this stage water molecules are split to produce oxygen, which is then released back into the atmosphere through the stomata under the leaves.

... AND DARK

Away from the light, the ATP is used to provide energy in the dark reaction (also known as the Calvin cycle), which converts carbon dioxide into glucose. Some glucose is used by the plant cells to carry out their normal functions. The rest is converted into a more complex sugar called starch, which can be stored. Starch can be turned back into glucose when the plant needs it.

in every square millimeter of leaf.

Requirements *for* LIFE

THE ESSENTIALS OF LIFE are very simple. All organisms need energy, water, shelter, and space *to grow*. The majority of life forms also need oxygen, nutrients, and a comfortable range of temperatures.

ENERGY

Without energy all living things would not be able to grow or function. The primary source of energy on Earth is light from the Sun. Animals cannot use it directly but plants and a few other organisms, such as green algae, are able to capture it and use it to make food. Plants are eaten by animals and these animals become food for carnivores (animals that only eat meat) and omnivores (animals that eat both plants and meat).

WATER

All living things need water. Cells are mostly made of water, and water plays a key role in moving vital substances in and out of the cell. Some organisms can survive with very little water. Desert-dwelling plants and animals, such as cacti and camels, have mechanisms that help them cope with drought and capture as much water as possible when it is available. By contrast, fish and other aquatic animals spend their whole life in water.

SHELTER

HOME SWEET HOME!

At some point in their lives, most animals search out somewhere for shelter (see pp.60–61). They do this to avoid predators or bad weather, to go to sleep, or to give birth to their young in safety. Without shelter, they could die from exposure or become dinner for another animal. Plants aren't so lucky—because they can't move they have to find different ways to tough out the weather and fend off animals that want to eat them.

LIVING SPACE

Everything needs a certain amount of space to live and grow. How much varies enormously. Bacteria can thrive in the tiniest of spaces, while a Siberian tiger needs around 120 sq. miles (300 sq. km) of territory in which to roam. If there is not enough space, populations become overcrowded, compete for food, water, and mates, and disease spreads quickly throughout the species.

This is MY space!

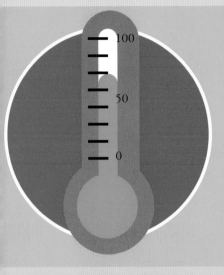

TEMPERATURE

Earth has a variety of climates ranging from very hot around the equator to freezing cold at the poles. Despite these extremes, life still manages to exist in these places. Antarctica can get as cold as –76°F (–60°C)—that's four times as cold as your freezer!—yet emperor penguins spend months incubating their eggs there and life has been found deep below the ice of Lake Vostok. At the other end of the scale, temperatures can climb to 140°F (60°C) across North African deserts where animals and plants manage to thrive.

NUTRIENTS

We all rely on these essential chemicals to build and repair body tissues, carry out vital functions, and produce energy. Animals obtain nutrients by eating food. Plants take them in from soil and the atmosphere through their roots and leaves. Bacteria absorb them directly through their cell membrane. A lack of nutrients can lead to problems—not enough vitamin C, for example, can cause a disease called scurvy in humans. So eat your fruit!

OXYGEN

All forms of animal life need oxygen. The only exceptions are some bacteria that can survive in oxygenless environments, such as inside a cow's stomach. Almost all the oxygen in the atmosphere is made by plants as part of a process known as photosynthesis. Plants take in carbon dioxide to make food and release oxygen back out into the atmosphere. So that nice flower in your window box is also helping you breathe.

The VARIETY of life

The *earliest forms of life* were nothing more than single cells, so where did the 8.7 million species of plants and animals that we share our planet with come from? And *why are they all so different?* The answer lies in a process called evolution, where organisms adapt over generations to their surroundings by *developing new features* and characteristics that help them survive.

Six kingdoms

EUBACTERIA

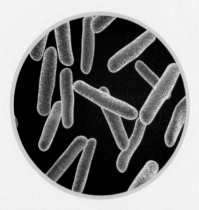

Types of organism: Simple single-celled bacteria
Distribution: Worldwide

Bacteria are found in all environments and conditions. They range from the cyanobacteria (blue-green algae), that first put oxygen into Earth's atmosphere, to organisms that cause diseases, such as typhoid or cholera. Useful types of bacteria can turn milk into yogurt or dirty water into clean water.

ARCHAEBACTERIA

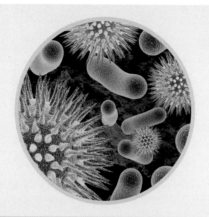

Types of organism: Simple single-celled bacteria
Distribution: Hostile environments

Archaebacteria are thought to be among the oldest types of living organisms on the planet. They survive in some of the most hostile conditions imaginable—boiling water, radioactive waste, and acid or alkaline pools—similar to those that existed when Earth first formed.

PROTISTS

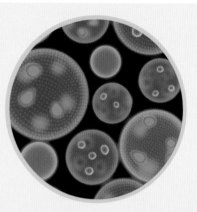

Types of organism: Slime molds, algae, protozoa
Distribution: Mainly marine or freshwater, sometimes land

Also known as the "odds and ends kingdom," members of the protist group are all different. They are microscopic organisms, but they are not bacteria, plants, fungi, or animals. Although they are single cells, they have a nucleus. They make their own food or feed on other organisms.

Splitting up the species

Kingdoms are very broad groups, so scientists split them up into smaller and smaller groups until they get to one single type of organism, which they call a species. They divide each group according to how similar or different the members are, and what they share in common. The classification for a lion looks like this:

KINGDOM	PHYLUM	CLASS	ORDER	FAMILY	GENUS	SPECIES
Animal	Chordates	Mammals	Carnivores	Cats	Big cats	Lion

To help us understand how life forms on the planet are related to each other, scientists organize them into six large groups called kingdoms. Once there were only two groups—animals and plants—but these were divided further after the discovery of invisible microscopic organisms.

FUNGI

Types of organism: Mushrooms, molds, yeasts
Distribution: Worldwide

Fungi used to be classed as plants until scientists discovered that they cannot make their own food. Instead they gain their energy by breaking down dead plants and animals. They consist of complex single or multiple cells and are chemically and genetically closer to animals than to plants.

PLANTS

Types of organism: Green algae, mosses, conifers, flowering plants
Distribution: Worldwide, though fewer in polar areas

Plants are multicelled complex organisms that can make their own food. They range from tiny mosses to enormous trees and have managed to colonize most areas of the world, including the oceans. Plants play a vital role in oxygenating the atmosphere.

ANIMALS

Types of organism: Insects, fish, mammals, crustaceans, reptiles, amphibians
Distribution: Worldwide

Animals range from the very simple—with no brain, no nervous system, and no spinal cord, such as a sponge—to highly complex mammals like ourselves. Animals can't make their own food, so they must obtain it by eating members of the other kingdoms.

We know our place— **king and queen** of the *cat family.*

So many SPECIES

EVOLUTION AND VARIATION

The reason why there are so many species is evolution. Evolution is a process of change that happens gradually over millions of years. Tiny alterations in the way an organism looks or behaves may give it an edge over other members of its species in its ability to survive. Sometimes new features are adapted and passed down through succeeding generations until the descendent looks or behaves differently from its ancestor. Then it may be classed as a new species.

> I COULD BE AN ELEPHANT ONE DAY!

MOERITHERIUM

GOMPHOTHERIUM

Natural selection

Adaptations make it easier for organisms to make use of a unique place in their ecosystem. That way, similar species can live together without competing for the same resources. Two related birds might not be able to live in the same tree if they both need the same type of food, but if one has a short bill suitable for eating insects and the other has a sharp bill for eating fruit then they can share a habitat. If they both fed on insects then the species that was better at catching them would eventually push the other species out. This process, where the best adapted survives, is called natural selection.

Sharp-billed fruit eater

Short-billed insect eater

GREEN HONEYCREEPER

SCARLET TANAGER

> They didn't find me until 2008, and haven't yet properly classified me!

This long-nosed frog is also called "Pinocchio". Scientists don't know if it is a new species of *Litoria* or not.

Voyage of discovery

Even though humans have visited everywhere on land there are still many places that haven't been properly explored. Even less is known about the ocean because of the difficulties of exploring in deep water. Scientists think that there could be as many as a million species in the sea and that we have only discovered 20 percent of them so far.

There are millions of different species living on Earth. In fact, there are so many we have hardly started counting them all. Scientists think there could be anything between 2 and 100 million, although the current best estimate is 8.7 million. Out of these, only 1.8 million have been named and described.

The elephant's trunk is actually a combined nose and upper lip that lengthened over the course of millions of years as its incisor teeth grew larger and turned into tusks. With such large tusks they needed a long trunk to be able to reach food easily. Those with the longest trunks survived best.

MAMMOTH

ELEPHANT

How many of each?

The largest number of named species belongs to the animal kingdom. This is followed by plants, fungi, and protists. We can only guess at the number of bacteria species but they probably run into *millions*.

Animals	1,471,428
Plants	307,674
Fungi and protists	51,623

End of the line

When the last of a species dies out it is said to be extinct. Extinction is a natural event—around 99 percent of the species that have ever lived on Earth are extinct. Most extinctions go unnoticed, but there have been five occasions in history when a large number of species were wiped out at the same time. These were the result of natural events—asteroids hitting Earth, extreme volcanic eruptions, or climate change. Scientists think we are now losing species so fast that we are facing a new extinction event caused by habitat loss, pollution, and hunting. This time the blame lies closer to home—human activity.

New species

Discoveries of new species are being made every year. In 2006 alone, it was estimated that 50 new species were being reported every day. The majority of these are small invertebrates, although a surprising number of mammals, amphibians, and reptiles are also found. There are also many species we already know about that need to be properly classifed and named. It takes time to work out whether something really is new or simply a variation of an existing species.

This giant woolly rat was discovered on an expedition to Papua New Guinea in 2009.

Evolution of life

Let's turn 4.6 billion years of evolution into one day...

Life on Earth began around 3.5 billion years ago. For many long years, life consisted of little more than single-celled organisms surviving in challenging conditions. Gradually, things began to change—animals and plants moved out of the water and onto the land. It's difficult to imagine just how long it took to arrive at the plants and animals we see today, but if you think of it in terms of a day humans didn't emerge until nearly midnight!

00:00　01:00　02:00　03:00　04:00　05:00　06:00　07:00　08:00　09:00　10:0

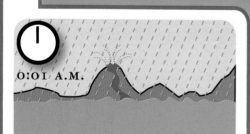

0:01 A.M.

GETTING STARTED

Earth forms. It is little more than a hot rock with a poisonous atmosphere. As it cools, the molten surface hardens to form a solid crust. At some point it starts raining and the oceans form.

4,600 million years ago

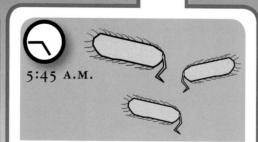

5:45 A.M.

FIRST LIFE

Conditions are still hostile, but simple prokaryote cells have begun to emerge in the ocean. Some of these are blue-green algae (cyanobacteria) that gradually oxygenate the water and the atmosphere.

3,500 million years ago

For the first three billion years, not a lot happened!

On this time scale, *every minute* is equivalent to *3.2 million years*.

1,500 million years ago

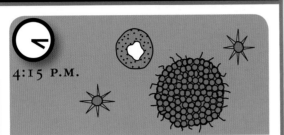

4:15 P.M.

GETTING COMPLICATED

Multicellular life forms emerge. Some of these will go on to be the ancestors of all plants, fungi, and animals. There's not much land above the waves so life stays in the water, but there's lots more oxygen in the atmosphere.

700 million years ago

8:20 P.M.

SNOWBALL EARTH

Lichens and simple plants start to grow inland. Unfortunately the climate turns extremely chilly and the whole planet becomes a snowball. A few hardy species survive on land and in deep water.

11:00 12:00 13:00 14:00 15:00 16:00 17:00 18:00 19:00 20:00 21:00

2:25 P.M.

COMPLEX CELLS

The first complex eukaryotes appear. It's still hard for life to survive outside of the water because of the deadly effect of the Sun's radiation. Protective ozone starts to build up in the atmosphere.

1,850 million years ago

5:40 P.M.

MOVING OUT

Organisms begin to get a bit more adventurous. Fungi and multicelled green algae venture out of the shallows to the fringes of the land. Life's a beach.

1,200 million years ago

8:35 P.M.

A SOFT LIFE

As things warm up again, a whole new set of soft-bodied animals evolve that are larger and more diverse than before. These include primitive sponges and jellyfish.

630 million years ago

Evolution of life *continues...*

540 million years ago

9:05 P.M.

ARMED FOR BATTLE

Suddenly thousands of new invertebrates burst onto the scene. An evolutionary arms race begins as species acquire hard shells, teeth, eyes, spines, guts, and feet. It's eat or be eaten now.

380 million years ago

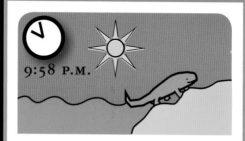

9:58 P.M.

ON THEIR TOES

Fish prop themselves up on their fins to breathe in air and develop a new skill—walking. Some set up home on land as the first amphibians. Crawling insects also move onto land.

300 million years ago

10:20 P.M.

TOUGH SHELLS

Growing a dry, scaly skin and making a tough, leathery shell for their eggs enables some amphibians to breed on land. They turned into reptiles.

21:00   22:00

9:12 P.M.

BONY BODIES

The first vertebrate animals appear in the form of jawless fish. Simple skeletons can support a muscly body that allows faster movement and much bigger body sizes.

530 million years ago

9:37 P.M.

HEADING OUT

Simple land plants begin to put down roots and a few brave crabs and scorpions start to investigate drier surroundings. This is a wise move since fish now have jaws!

450 million years ago

10:12 P.M.

IN THE TREETOPS

Plants start to get bigger and forests of primitive trees grow in swamps around the coast. Some develop seeds and spread farther inland. Insects evolve wings and take to the skies.

350 million years ago

After 9 p.m., *evolution* really began to *speed up!*

155 million years ago

11:06 P.M.

TAKING TO THE SKIES

A group of feathered dinosaurs learn how to fly and evolve into birds. Sharks, reptiles, and amphibians start to look like their modern forms and insects begin to pollinate flowering plants.

250,000 years ago

11:59 P.M.

LAST OF THE LINE

Homo sapiens, or modern man, emerges from a long line of early humans that have learned to stand and walk on two feet. He co-exists with Neanderthals, another human species, until they inexplicably die out 25,000 years ago.

23:00

24:00

10:42 P.M.

MONSTER REPTILES

The planet is full of reptiles—they fly, they swim, they make the ground shake. This is the time of the dinosaurs, some of which become enormous. Flowering plants, conifers, cycads, and ferns provide them with giant bushes to lurk in.

240 million years ago

10:43 P.M.

RISE OF THE MAMMALS

The combination of a huge asteroid hitting the earth and volcanic activity wipe out the dinosaurs and provide an opportunity for tiny mammals to take over. The first line of human ancestors start to diverge from apes.

65 million years ago

VASCULAR PLANTS

The majority of plants are vascular and include ferns, conifers, and flowering plants. Most reproduce using seeds, which grow inside a flower, fruit, or cone (see pp.80–81). Vascular plants can grow tall because their cell walls contain a stiffening compound called lignin.

Growing up

There are more than **300,000 species** of plants on Earth. Without them, there would never have been enough OXYGEN in the atmosphere or the seas to *support animal life*. Plants thrive everywhere except for the icy poles, the dry deserts, and the deep oceans.

Flowering plants

are the most diverse group with 268,000 known species. A quarter of these belong to just three families—the orchids, the peas, and the sunflowers.

Conifers

are woody plants with long, narrow, or scale-like leaves. Their seeds grow inside a protective cone before being dropped to the ground. Conifers include pines, cedars, firs, and redwoods.

Ferns

are leafy plants with stems, leaves, and roots, but which reproduce using spores. There are around 12,000 species of fern, including horsetails, snake-tongued ferns, and whisk ferns.

Bud

Petal

Stem

Leaf

Root

Mmm, this sugar-making leaf tastes so sweet!

Every part of a flowering plant, like this hibiscus, has a special function to help it grow: the leaves produce food, the roots suck up water, and the flowers hold the seeds for reproduction.

Green

Plants are divided into two groups according to how they absorb water and how they reproduce. Plants that take in water from the soil through their roots are called vascular plants. They have special cells that run the length of their stem and allow them to pull water up to the top of the plant.

Non-vascular plants have to absorb water through their leaves because they *don't have true roots or stems*. They need to live in damp places, otherwise they would DRY OUT too quickly.

NON-VASCULAR PLANTS

Non-vascular plants include mosses, worts, and a mainly freshwater group of green algae called Chlorophyta. They don't have flowers and they reproduce using spores. Without the specialized tissue of vascular plants, they do not generally grow tall.

Mosses
are low-growing, small-leaved plants. They have hardly any roots to anchor them and have to take in water through their leaves. The spores are carried in a capsule suspended above the plant by a stalk.

Worts
have a ribbon-like plant body called a thallus or are arranged as a series of overlapping, segmented leaves. They are usually less than 4 in (10 cm) long and bear their spores on stalks.

Green algae
vary greatly in size from tiny single cells to large seaweeds. They grow wherever there is water—even on ice and snow. To reproduce, they spread their spores by air or water.

Inside a stem

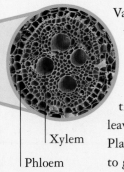

Vascular plants have two sets of tubes running through their stems. The xylem transports water and minerals from the roots to the leaves and flowers. The phloem transports sugars made in the leaves to the rest of the plant. Plants use these essential nutrients to grow and reproduce.

Xylem

Phloem

Things that
COME UP *in the night*

IT'S A BIT OF AN ANIMAL

For many years, scientists classed fungi as part of the plant kingdom. In fact, they are closer to animals. The cell walls of fungi are made of chitin, which is found in the shells of insects and crustaceans. They also store food as glycogen, a carbohydrate found in the muscles and liver of animals. Plants, by contrast, have cell walls made of cellulose and store food as starch.

> Never eat a wild mushroom that hasn't been identified as safe by an expert!

Anatomy of a fungus

You rarely see all of a fungus since most of it lies underground. Most grow as long, thin filaments called hyphae that form a mesh, or mycelium, which threads through the soil. Only the bits that carry the spores emerge above ground as mushrooms and toadstools. They consist of a stalk and a cap, sac, or cup, with gills underneath that contain the spores.

Cap

Gills

Veil

Stalk

Mycelium

Toadstool emerges

Cap develops

Mushrooms

Mushrooms and toadstools are the fruiting bodies of underground fungi and come in a wide variety of shapes, resembling umbrellas, pancakes, puffballs, or shrivelled fruits. Some mushrooms, such as morels and truffles, can be eaten and are a good source of protein—and delicious! But other species, like the Jack O'Lantern, are extremely poisonous. Others produce vivid colors that can be used to dye textiles and paper.

Fungi cannot make their own food so they get it from the soil or by breaking down dead matter. Saprophytes are fungi that secrete enzymes to extract the nutrients they need. Other types of fungi are parasitic—they get their nutrients by growing on a living host, such as a tree. The tree gains extra nutrients from the fungus's mycelium and the fungus gets food from the tree.

The veins in blue cheese *are caused by molds*

Fungi and related members of their kingdom are magical organisms—they seem to spring from nowhere overnight. This happens because their microscopic spores are all around us. Mushrooms are actually more likely to appear after rain, which provides good conditions for spores to germinate. The best place to find them is among fallen leaves in temperate woodland.

BRACKET FUNGUS   **JACK O'LANTERN**   **PARASOL**   **MOREL**

Molds

Molds are microscopic fungi. Their spores are everywhere and germinate very quickly, sending out a mesh of white hyphae through a new food source. When they are ready to reproduce they make colored spores that may be pink, blue, gray, black, or green and appear powdery.

Yeasts

Yeasts are single-celled fungi that live in colonies and absorb nutrients through their cell wall. Most live in liquid environments that are naturally rich in sugar, such as the nectar of flowers. Some yeasts, when fermented, convert carbohydrates to carbon dioxide (used in baking) and alcohol (used in beer brewing).

Lichens

Lichens are really two organisms that live together—a fungus and an alga. The alga lives inside the fungus's tissues, which protect it from the outside world and provides it with water and nutrients. In return, the alga makes starch by photosynthesis and some of it is used by the fungus. This relationship allows the lichen to survive in tough places, such as on bare desert rocks. Unlike other fungi, lichens grow very slowly—some are hundreds of years old.

> *The biggest living thing is a fungus. It extends more than 3.8 sq. miles (10 sq. km) under a forest in Oregon and is thought to be 8,500 years old.*

growing in the cracks but they are perfectly *edible.*

All CREATURES great ...

More than 1.3 MILLION SPECIES of animals have been described and named—and there are even more waiting to be discovered. Here are a few of the groups of animals that have a backbone (vertebrates) and, on the next page, those that don't (invertebrates).

MAMMALS
Number of species: 5,513

KEY FEATURES		Give birth to live young		Feed young on milk		Have hair or fur		Warm-blooded

Mammals were the last group of animals to evolve. They are an extremely diverse group that live on land and in the sea. Although the majority give birth to well-developed young, two families lay eggs—the platypus and the echidnas; these are known as monotremes. Marsupials, such as kangaroos and koalas, produce undeveloped young, which live in their mother's pouch until they can fend for themselves. Mammals eat meat (carnivores), plants (herbivores), or a mixed diet (omnivores).

KANGAROO

HUMAN

RABBIT

ZEBRA

DOG

BIRDS
Number of species: 10,425

KEY FEATURES		Lay eggs		Covered in feathers		Most fly		Warm-blooded

Birds evolved during the time of the dinosaurs, to which they are closely related. Their feathers are warm and waterproof and they have scaly, clawed feet. Instead of teeth they have a hard bill that is specialized for the type of food that they eat. All birds have wings, but not all can fly. A lightweight skeleton makes flying easier. In some birds, such as the penguin, the wings have been adapted for swimming, while most non-flying land birds use their wings for balance or display.

OSTRICH

SCARLET IBIS

MACAW   ROBIN   SWAN   PENGUIN

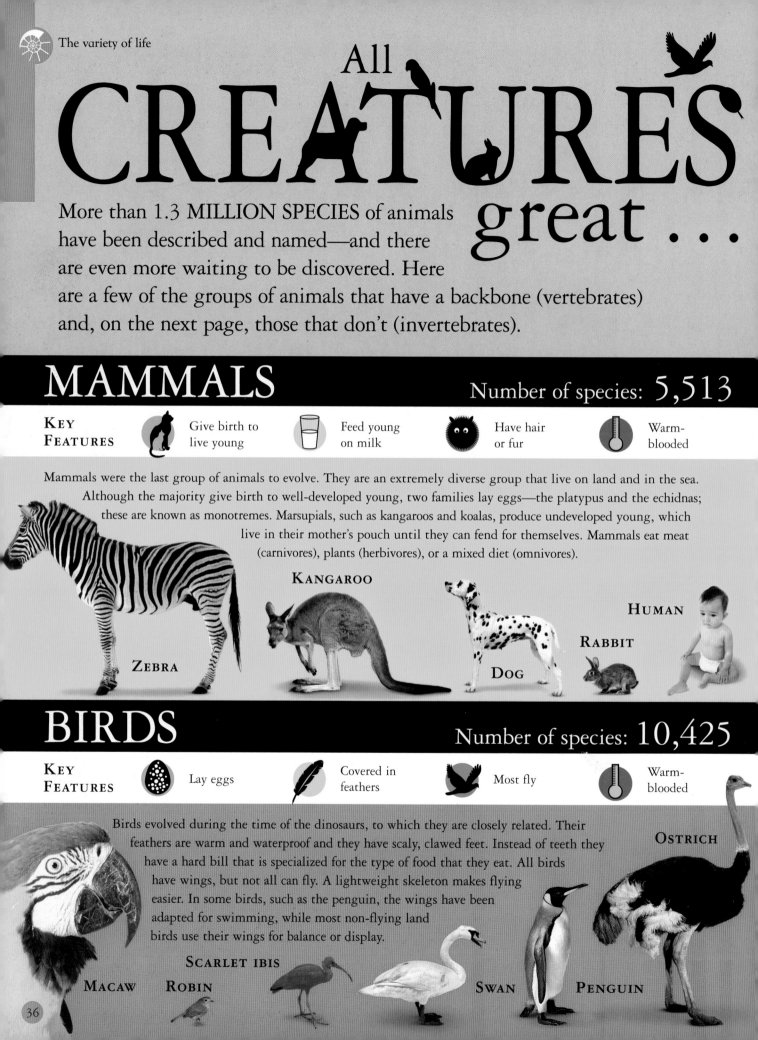

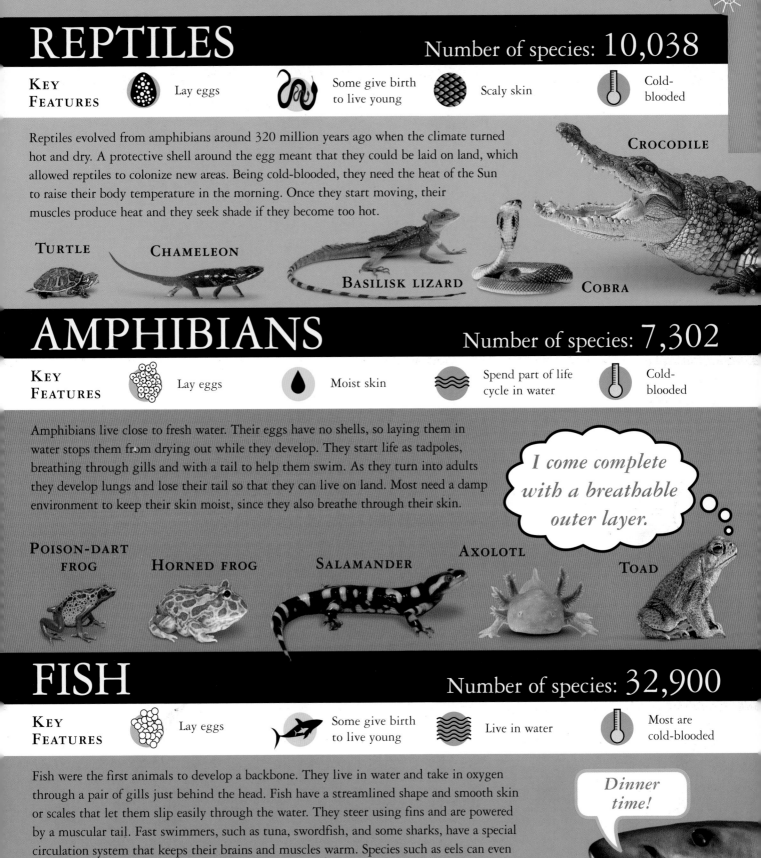

REPTILES

Number of species: 10,038

KEY FEATURES — Lay eggs — Some give birth to live young — Scaly skin — Cold-blooded

Reptiles evolved from amphibians around 320 million years ago when the climate turned hot and dry. A protective shell around the egg meant that they could be laid on land, which allowed reptiles to colonize new areas. Being cold-blooded, they need the heat of the Sun to raise their body temperature in the morning. Once they start moving, their muscles produce heat and they seek shade if they become too hot.

CROCODILE

TURTLE   CHAMELEON   BASILISK LIZARD   COBRA

AMPHIBIANS

Number of species: 7,302

KEY FEATURES — Lay eggs — Moist skin — Spend part of life cycle in water — Cold-blooded

Amphibians live close to fresh water. Their eggs have no shells, so laying them in water stops them from drying out while they develop. They start life as tadpoles, breathing through gills and with a tail to help them swim. As they turn into adults they develop lungs and lose their tail so that they can live on land. Most need a damp environment to keep their skin moist, since they also breathe through their skin.

I come complete with a breathable outer layer.

POISON-DART FROG   HORNED FROG   SALAMANDER   AXOLOTL   TOAD

FISH

Number of species: 32,900

KEY FEATURES — Lay eggs — Some give birth to live young — Live in water — Most are cold-blooded

Fish were the first animals to develop a backbone. They live in water and take in oxygen through a pair of gills just behind the head. Fish have a streamlined shape and smooth skin or scales that let them slip easily through the water. They steer using fins and are powered by a muscular tail. Fast swimmers, such as tuna, swordfish, and some sharks, have a special circulation system that keeps their brains and muscles warm. Species such as eels can even live on the land for short periods of time.

Dinner time!

GOLDFISH   ANGELFISH   LIONFISH   EEL   SHARK

...and SMALL

Around 97 percent of animals are INVERTEBRATES—creatures without a backbone. Not only that, they don't have a bony skeleton or proper jaws either. Instead, many rely on a hard outer covering (exoskeleton) to support their body, or have a shell for protection. There are more than 30 large groups of invertebrates—here are a few that you may have come across.

INSECTS
Number of species: more than 1,100,000

KEY FEATURES	Paired jointed legs	Compound eyes	Hard exoskeleton	Many have wings

Insects are the largest and probably the most successful group of animals on Earth. They were the first organisms to fly, which enabled them to colonize many new environments. When insects emerge from the egg, some, for example butterflies, have a completely different body structure from their adult form. They have to go through a stage called metamorphosis, where their body is broken down and reassembled. Others, such as grasshoppers, go through a process of splitting off their exoskeleton as they grow bigger.

LADYBUGS

BEETLE   CENTIPEDE   BUTTERFLY   MOTH   STICK INSECT

CRUSTACEANS
Number of species: 47,000

KEY FEATURES	Jointed legs	Hard exoskeleton

Crustaceans are mainly found in the water, although wood lice live on land. Crustaceans are related to insects but have a less obviously segmented body. Some segments are fused together to form a single piece, which gives better protection for their eyes and head. Although lobsters and crabs have menacing claws, these are used for defense rather than attacking prey. Most feed on the remains of other animals or particles floating through the water.

SPIDER CRAB

LOBSTER   HERMIT CRAB

SHRIMP   WOOD LOUSE

ARACHNIDS

Number of species: 102,248

KEY FEATURES Eight legs — Many make webs

Arachnids are found on land or in fresh water. Their body is divided into two segments—a fused head and thorax and an abdomen. They are mainly carnivorous, pouring digestive enzymes from their stomach over their food before sucking it up into their mouth. Many of them are hunters. Spiders spin webs of silk to trap prey; they also inject prey with venom, as do scorpions. Many arachnids have fine sensory hairs on their body that gives them a sense of touch.

TARANTULA

MITE

TRAP-DOOR SPIDER

ORB WEAVER SPIDER

SCORPION

MOLLUSKS

Number of species: 85,000

KEY FEATURES Soft body — Unsegmented — Some have shells

Mollusks are a diverse group of organisms with a wide variety of body shapes. Many have a hard outer shell for protection and to support the body. They have a nervous system and a primitive brain, although in octopuses and squid the brain is highly developed. They have tiny toothlike structures called denticles, which they use to scrape algae off rocks or to bore through shells into the flesh of other mollusks. Members of the octopus family are free swimmers—scallops can use jet propulsion. Other mollusks move around on the seabed using a single muscular foot.

GIANT AFRICAN SNAIL

OCTOPUS

LETTUCE SLUG

SCALLOP

GIANT CLAM

CNIDARIANS

Number of species: 11,300

KEY FEATURES Soft body Swim by pushing water out of body cavity

Cnidarians are found only in water, and the water supports their body. They can detect light, but don't actually have eyes. Instead they rely on their senses of smell and touch to detect prey and predators. Many are equipped with stinging cells on their tentacles that inject venom and digestive enzymes. Anemones and corals are mainly filter feeders, trapping particles of food with their arms.

ANEMONE

BRAIN CORAL

RED CORAL

DEAD MAN'S FINGERS CORAL

JELLYFISH

Teeny tiny WORLD

Most organisms on the planet are invisible to us, but if you were to look at a cubic inch of air, water, or soil with a microscope you would find it bursting with life. We call these tiny life forms microorganisms, or microbes. They include plants, animals, fungi, protists, and all bacteria.

Microscopes have become more and more powerful; now we can see up to a magnification of 500,000 times with a scanning electron microscope.

Microbes are like other living things—some make their own food and some have to eat other organisms. They live on their own or in colonies in every kind of environment: on land, in water, and in the air. Some, called archaebacteria, survive in the most hostile places on the planet—hot springs, acid pools, and deep in the ground—places that would be deadly to other life forms.

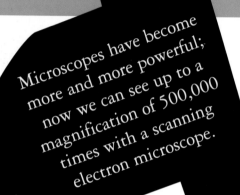

BACTERIA

I've just spotted an *animalcule!*

ANTON VAN LEEUWENHOEK

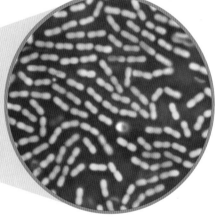

Now you see them...

Even though they could not be seen, for centuries people believed that microorganisms existed and that they could be the cause of disease. It was not until the invention of the microscope in the 17th century that it became obvious just how many microorganisms there were. A Dutch scientist, Anton van Leeuwenhoek, known as the "Father of Microbiology," was the first to observe what he called "animalcules."

Bacteria

Bacteria are simple single-celled microbes. The largest bacteria are around half a millimeter long, but still only just visible with the naked eye. They are mainly spherical or rod-shaped, with longer rods sometimes twisted into spirals. Some species form chains, clusters, or dense mats. Bacteria can be useful or harmful.

Good bacteria turn milk into cheese and yogurt, treat sewage, help cows digest grass, and fix nitrogen in the soil.

YOGURT BACTERIA

Bad bacteria cause diseases in animals and plants, contaminate water, and poison food.

E.COLI BACTERIA

Protozoa

These are the most advanced form of microbes and belong to the protist kingdom. Many have features that are not found in bacteria, such as a whip-like tail, hairs, or foot-like projections (called pseudopods) that pull them along. They prey on bacteria, single-celled algae, and microfungi. Protozoa are also responsible for diseases such as malaria.

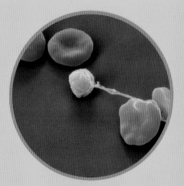

MALARIA PROTOZOAN

Fungi

Most people think of fungi as mushrooms but there are many other species that are too small to see. Some cause diseases such as athlete's foot or ringworm in humans or blight in plants. Yeasts are used to make bread and soy sauce, and molds make the blue veins in cheese. Fungi are also used to make antibiotics that kill bacteria.

BLUE-CHEESE MOLD

Plankton

The majority of living organisms in the oceans today are bacteria. These, along with other microscopic animals, larvae, and plants, are known as plankton. They are concentrated in the well-lit surface layers of the oceans and provide food for larger animals. The name "plankton" comes from the Greek word for drifter, or wanderer, since the organisms drift along with the current.

PLANKTON

MICRO QUIZ

Can you *guess* what these are? *Read the clues:*

 1 Beautifully colored scales help this insect fly and flutter. They usually look smooth and delicate.

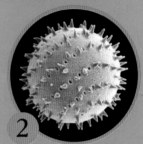 2 If you get hayfever you may not like these, but plants couldn't reproduce without them.

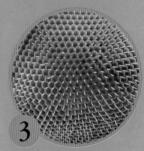 3 Made up of hundreds of facets, this is a very useful organ. The tiny animal that uses it is hard to catch.

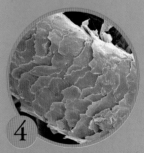 4 This shaft of dead and flattened cells helps protect us. It grows up to 0.3 mm every day.

 5 Who would guess that these soft and delicate parts of a plant would look so bumpy close up?

Answers: 1. Butterfly wing, 2. pollen grain, 3. fly eye, 4. human hair, 5. flower petal.

Living TOGETHER

There are *so many species* that our planet could seem rather full. Luckily, we don't all want to *live in the same places* or *eat the same things*. However, that doesn't mean that every organism lives in harmony with its neighbors. *Life can be very competitive*, even among members of the same species. Despite this, everything on Earth is part of a *close-knit community*—if one species vanishes it can affect *the whole ecosystem*.

WORLD *of* PLENTY

Every square inch of our planet is occupied by some form of life.
From the highest mountaintops to the depths of the oceans, something
has found exactly what it needs to survive and make a life there.

WHO LIVES WHERE

Although organisms are found everywhere on Earth, more species live in tropical regions
than at the poles. Climate and abundance of food are the main factors affecting how
many and what type of species live there.

CLIMATE

Arctic

It's hard for plants and
fungi to survive the cold,
so animals and bacteria
are the main species.

Northern hemisphere

Warmer temperatures
and more rain mean
more plants, fungi, and
a wider range of animals.

The equator

The warm, wet, sunny tropics
are attractive to plants, which
make them an ideal habitat for
all sorts of living things. These
areas have the most species.

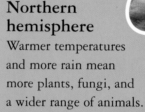

Southern hemisphere

A wide range of plants
and animals live here,
and its oceans are
full of species.

Antarctic

There are few plants, but
animals and birds use the
firm land under the ice
as a breeding ground.

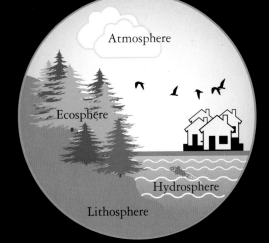

THE BIOSPHERE

Scientists call the living world the biosphere. It extends from the upper reaches of the atmosphere to the deepest trenches in the ocean and far below the surface of the land. The biosphere is where all the other "spheres"— the atmosphere (air), the hydrosphere (water), the lithosphere (land), and the ecosphere (living things), meet and interact with each other.

BIODIVERSITY

We call the variety of plants, animals, and microorganisms in an area its biodiversity. If an area has good physical conditions, such as in the tropics, then it will have a high diversity of animals and plants because it has plenty of resources to support the growth of living things. Areas with poorer conditions have fewer plant species and a limited range of animals.

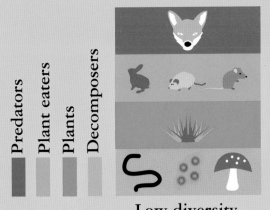

Predators | Plant eaters | Plants | Decomposers

Low diversity

Medium diversity

High diversity

Teeming with life

Some places are extremely rich in species and are known as hotspots. Many of the plants and animals in a hotspot are found only in that area. Hotspots are valuable because the wide variety of species makes them a potential source of new medicines, crops, and even ideas for technology. The downside is that such a large number of species makes these regions attractive to humans and many are now under threat from loss of habitat and overuse of their resources. Parts of the ocean also have hotspots, which makes them popular fishing grounds.

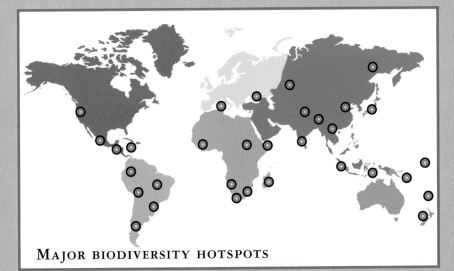

MAJOR BIODIVERSITY HOTSPOTS

Part *of the* SYSTEM

No organism lives entirely alone. As well as all the living things around it—plants, animals, bacteria, and fungi—it interacts with the air, soil, water, and sunlight. We call such a group of organisms a **community** and, together with the environment it lives in, an **ecosystem**.

ECOSYSTEMS

Ecosystems can be as small as a crack in a rock or as big as Earth itself. Really large ecosystems are called biomes and consist of many smaller ecosystems. Each ecosystem is made up of a number of habitats. A habitat is the place where one or more species live. The habitat must be able to supply everything the organism needs or it will go somewhere more suitable.

FOX

INSECT

Ideal habitat

A tree provides a habitat for many species, including birds, insects, and mammals. Birds roost on branches, eat insects, and make nests to raise their young. Mammals might burrow among the tree's roots and eat nuts and seeds. Insects eat leaves and lay eggs on them. The tree relies on the bird to get rid of pests and the mammal to spread its seeds. Each organism has a different use for the tree, but they all interact with, and depend on, the other species that live there.

BIRD

Finding your niche

Every organism has a way of life that is unique to its species. While many species may share a habitat, each has its own role in the community called a niche. For example, a forest may provide the habitat for a fox. Its niche is that of a predator eating smaller animals that also live in the forest. Out on a prairie, a coyote occupies the same predator niche as a fox. However, you would never find a fox and a coyote trying to occupy the same niche in the same habitat. There wouldn't be enough food for both species to survive.

FOREST

Always changing

Ecosystems change over time. A piece of bare soil may eventually become a forest as new plants take root and attract animals that feed on them. They, in turn, attract predators. The ecosystem gradually becomes more complex as more species come in to fill new gaps. Eventually the ecosystem matures and reaches a balance point where all the things that live there have exactly what they need to survive.

Fox in residence!

RABBITS

GOOD-BYE!

COYOTE

RECYCLING

One of the key functions of an ecosystem is to recycle energy, water, and nutrients. Recycling is a vital process. If any of the substances needed for life became locked up in a form where they couldn't be used, life would eventually grind to a halt. Some of these cycles can take millions of years to complete, others as little as a day.

The carbon cyle

The carbon cycle is a good example of how essential elements are recycled. Plants take carbon dioxide out of the atmosphere to use in photosynthesis (see pp.18–19). Animals eat the plants and build the carbon into their muscles. They also breathe carbon dioxide back into the air. Dead animals and plants are broken down by decomposers, which release the carbon back into the soil.

SUNLIGHT

Carbon cycle

Too much extra carbon dioxide can unbalance the natural carbon cycle.

Cars and factories burn fossil fuels for energy, releasing carbon dioxide into the atmosphere.

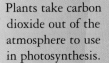

Plants take carbon dioxide out of the atmosphere to use in photosynthesis.

Animals breathe out carbon dioxide and return it to the atmosphere.

Plants also release carbon dioxide at night.

Dead plants rot and are buried. Eventually they become fossil fuels.

Dead organisms and their wastes are broken down by decomposers and carbon is returned to the soil.

Plant roots put carbon back into the soil.

Crabs use carbon compounds to build their shells.

In the ocean

Living things are constantly breathing carbon dioxide back into the atmosphere. Human activity, mainly through burning fossil fuels, is also adding vast amounts. Not all of this carbon dioxide remains in the air—some dissolves in the oceans and lakes, and some is used by aquatic plants for photosynthesis. Carbon is also used by marine animals to build their shells or skeletons. In time, the empty shells build up to form a rock called limestone.

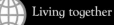

Life *zones*

LIFE ON EARTH can be organized into a number of *large ecosystems,* or biomes. *Biomes* are based on geographic regions that have similar climates (how hot or cold, windy or rainy a place is). You can find the same type of biome on different continents and in different hemispheres but the *animal and plant species* in each one varies widely.

TEMPERATE FOREST

Trees in this biome are broad-leaved varieties that drop their leaves in winter. There are distinct seasons and regular rainfall throughout the year. Animals that live in these areas feed mainly on seeds, nuts, leaves, and berries or are omnivores (they eat meat and plants).

TROPICAL FORESTS

The hot, wet, and sunny climate of tropical forests is ideal for tree growth. Most of the animals live in trees and there is always something in flower or fruit for them to eat throughout the year. This biome contains more species of plants, animals, and fungi than any other.

MOUNTAINS

Mountains are a mixture of habitats: their peaks can be cold, windy, and rocky with little plant life, but as you come down the slopes the landscape changes to bushes or conifers, then broadleaf trees. Valleys at the bottom are often very fertile and covered with meadows and forests.

TUNDRA

Tundra is the region around the southern edges of the Arctic Circle. It is covered with snow for much of the year, which melts during the spring and summer allowing small plants to grow. Animals that live here have a thick layer of fur or feathers and can store fat to keep them warm through the winter.

BOREAL FOREST

Boreal forest, or taiga, contains the world's tallest, toughest trees. Conifers thrive here because their needle-like leaves are strong and windproof, and allow snow to slide off. The top animals here are predatory mammals such as wolves, foxes, weasels, and wolverines.

DESERTS

Deserts are hot and extremely dry. Plants such as cacti have swollen stems or roots that can store water, and tiny leaves to prevent water loss. Desert animals can go for long periods without water, and some build burrows to esape the daytime heat.

GRASSLANDS

Natural grasslands are found on all continents—they get very hot in summer but don't have enough rainfall to support many trees or shrubs. Instead they are covered in grasses and plants that make ideal grazing for herds of plant-eating mammals. These, in turn, provide a meal for large carnivores such as lions.

My thick fur keeps me warm in the North Pole

POLAR

Ice, hurricane winds, freezing temperatures, and months of endless darkness make polar regions inhospitable to most land-dwelling species—those that live here migrate with the seasons. Yet the polar oceans are teeming with life, from microscopic plankton to the huge blue whale.

Unusual *alliances*

Getting along with your own species is one way of ensuring your survival. Another is to form a close alliance with another organism so that you both benefit. It really can pay to get along with your neighbors!

CLOSE FRIENDS

In some relationships between different species, only one half of the partnership benefits. The host species often provides food, a home, or transportation for the other species, but doesn't suffer any harm from it. This type of relationship is called commensalism.

Some say he's only using me as bait for a bigger fish, but I FEEL SO SAFE in his protective arms.

CLOWN FISH

SEA ANEMONE

It's great to catch the sun from up here. The view from this tree is SPECTACULAR.

ORCHID

TREE

This really is a comfy ride. And what's more, she NEVER COMPLAINS.

EMPEROR SHRIMP

SEA CUCUMBER

Clown fish make their home inside the tentacles of sea anemones. They are immune to the anemone's stings, which paralyze other fish, making it an ideal hiding place. The clown fish also benefits from scraps of food that the anemone misses. The anemone seems to get little more than some occasional cleaning, although the clown fish may act as bait for bigger fish.

Many orchids live high up on the branches of rainforest trees. They benefit by being much closer to the light than if they were on the forest floor. They cause no damage to the tree unless too many try to grow on it at the same time, when the weight may break the branches. They get all their water and nutrients from the air and rain, and sometimes from plant debris that accumulates on the branch.

Emperor shrimp live on sea slugs and sea cucumbers. They use them for shelter and transportation and feed on food disturbed by the host. It will even eat its host's poop. The shrimp also benefits from the poisonous reputation of sea slugs; predators avoid them. Emperor shrimp often change their color to match their host and camouflage themselves for extra protection.

Home to many

Sloths often look as if they have green fur because of the algae growing on their outer hairs. The algae camouflage the sloth among the leaves and provide it with extra nutrients that the sloth takes in while grooming its fur. This alga lives only on sloths. There is also a moth that lives on the sloth. It eats the algae and lays its eggs in the sloth's droppings. Several other insect species live in the fur, including mites and beetles.

SLOTH

I just love BOTH of them.

ALGAE

SLOTH MOTH

PERFECT PARTNERS

Sometimes a close relationship works to the benefit of both species. In some cases, the partners live separately, but gain from being together for a period of time. Others are more dependent and one may die without the other. This type of relationship is called mutualism.

I get all that yummy nectar and she gets the pollen. It's a WIN–WIN situation for both of us.

HONEY BEE

FLOWER

My live-in algal friends and I believe in GIVE and TAKE. But if things get tough, I'll kick them out!

CORAL

ALGAE

I used to hate going to the hygienist until I came here. They're always SO HAPPY to see me.

FISH

CLEANER WRASSE

Many flowering plants depend on insects, birds, and animals for pollination or to spread their seed. The animals are provided with food and, in turn, they help in the flower's reproductive process. Bees visit flowers to collect nectar and pollen. As they move from one flower to the next they transfer pollen, ensuring that the flower is fertilized and can set seed.

Corals and lichens both play host to algae, which live in their tissues. In return for shelter and vital nutrients, the algae provide their host with some of the sugars they make through photosynthesis. Not all corals share their living space with algae, but those that do regulate how many algae they take in. When the coral gets stressed it expels the algae, but if it tries to live without them for too long, it will die.

Many species of fish rely on others to rid them of lice, fungal infections, or dead skin. On coral reefs there are often cleaning stations where big fish line up for the attentions of smaller fish or shrimp. The big fish signals so the cleaner knows it is safe to approach. The cleaner then swims in and out of its client's mouth and gills in search of tasty morsels.

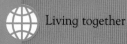

EAT *and be*

Every organism needs food to keep it going. Food provides energy that keeps cells working. Without energy, living things would not be able to move or breathe or grow.

You can't catch me…

PRODUCERS AND CONSUMERS

Organisms that make their own food are called **producers**. Plants are producers because they use the Sun's energy to make sugar. They do this by using what's around them—carbon dioxide, water, and sunlight. Animals cannot make their own food so they get energy from eating plants and other animals. They are **consumers**.

FOOD WEBS

DECREASING ENERGY

In a food chain, energy is passed from one link to the next, although some energy is lost with every link. When an herbivore eats a plant, some of the plant energy goes into the animal's muscles and organs and the rest is used to keep its body working. When a carnivore eats the herbivore, only the small amount of energy in the herbivore's muscles and organs is passed to the carnivore.

Energy-loss pyramid

At the bottom of this pyramid are plants and shrubs. In the middle are the herbivores. Right at the top is a single carnivore. It takes many herbivores to support one carnivore and millions of plants to support the herbivores.

Decreasing energy

Coyote

Mice

Grass

EATEN BY

Sun's Energy

Cacti

Grasses

Meadow herbs

Meadow flowers

Shrubs

Producers found on a prairie include grasses, meadow flowers, small shrubs, and cacti. They all make their own food.

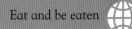

EATEN

Most organisms can't make their own food so they have to get it by eating something that can. This is the start of a food chain.

Oh yes I can! GULP!

There are rarely more than four or five links in each food chain. But most animals are part of several chains and eat more than one type of food to meet their energy needs. These interconnected food chains form a food web.

REGULATING THE CHAIN

Food chains have a way of balancing themselves out when the population of one of the links gets too large. Fewer mule deer could mean less food for the coyotes that eat them. However, if the coyotes starved and died, more mule deer would survive and reproduce.

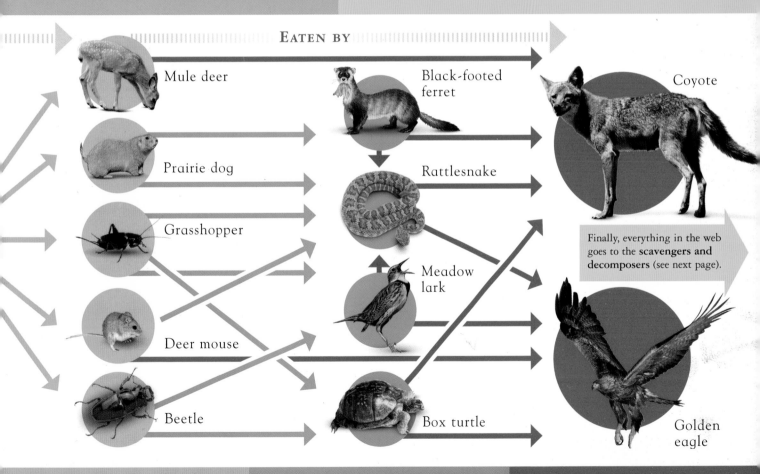

EATEN BY

Mule deer

Prairie dog

Grasshopper

Deer mouse

Beetle

Black-footed ferret

Rattlesnake

Meadow lark

Box turtle

Coyote

Finally, everything in the web goes to the **scavengers and decomposers** (see next page).

Golden eagle

Primary consumers are animals that eat plants—these are called herbivores. They help keep the vegetation at manageable levels.

Secondary consumers are animals that eat other animals—these are called carnivores. Most carnivores prey on herbivores or scavenge carcasses.

Tertiary consumers are at the top of the food chain. These are carnivores that eat other carnivores as well as herbivores.

The CLEAN

Every day millions of **plants and animals die.** Considering that organisms have been living and dying for billions of years, why are we not standing on a thick layer of dead

SCAVENGERS

Scavengers are animals that prefer to hunt for dead animals, or carrion, rather than catch live prey, although most carnivores will also eat dead meat. Scavengers rely on their acute sense of smell to find a carcass, sometimes from far away. They have sharp teeth or beaks and strong jaws that can rip a body open and crack bones. By breaking open the carcass they also make it easier for smaller scavengers, such as insects and crows, to nip in and grab a bite.

EARTHWORM

Plant scavengers

Not all scavengers eat animals. Earthworms pull fallen leaves into the soil and termites send out search parties to bring plant material back to their nest. The cellulose in plant cell walls is a rich source of energy but is indigestible to many animals. Plant scavengers break it down and excrete what they can't use into the soil.

GARDEN SNAIL

Leaves are YUMMY!

Sharp sight
Good for spying carcasses from high in the sky.

Vultures are *supremely adapted* for scavenging.

Bald head
No feathers to get covered in blood and guts.

Long neck
Useful for dipping deep inside a carcass.

SUPER SCAVENGER

Digestive juices
Strong enough to kill bacteria in rotting meat.

Sharp talons
For getting a grip on a carcass to tear it apart.

GRIFFON VULTURE

UP crew

Flies like a rotten place to lay their eggs.

bodies? The answer lies in a group of organisms whose way of life depends on the death of others. These are *nature's clean-up crew*—the scavengers and decomposers.

DECOMPOSERS

CHEMICAL CONVERTERS

Decomposers are a vital part of the food chain because they turn organic materials back into simple chemical nutrients, such as carbon, nitrogen, and oxygen. These are then released back into the air, soil, or water. It's easy to tell when decomposers are at work—they are responsible for many of the smells of rotting food and the slimy goo that is left behind.

Fungi

Fungi and molds can't make or catch their own food—instead they grow on dead plants and animals. They send out root-like structures (hyphae) that secrete enzymes that turn dead matter into nutrients.

Molds

Molds are a type of fungus that grow in colonies on rotting food. They spread across the surface in a network of white hyphae called a mycelium. Molds reproduce using gray, green, or brown spores.

Insects

Insects are vital decomposers. Many lay their eggs in rotting material, which hatch into maggots and grubs. These feed on the material, stripping carcasses to the bone and returning nutrients to the soil.

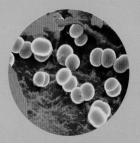

Bacteria

Bacteria are everywhere. Ninety percent of the microorganisms in a gram of soil are bacteria and between them they will digest almost anything. They bring about the final breakdown of substances.

The problem with poop...

NO JOB TOO SMALL

It isn't only dead bodies that need to be disposed rid of. Animals can't digest everything they eat, so they have to excrete it as waste along with dead cells from their own body. Luckily, one animal's poop is another organism's dinner, which is why we're not up to our eyeballs in the stuff. In fact, decomposers delight in animal waste because it is partially broken down and contains vital nutrients.

Dung lunch

Dung beetles eat, live, and breed in animal droppings and will even steal a precious ball of dung from another beetle. Some ride along on an animal, waiting for it to poop.

Sewage to fertilizer

Water and sewage treatment works take advantage of bacteria's taste for human waste, using them to turn sewage into clean water and fertilizer that can be spread onto fields.

KEEPING
the *balance*

There are two things that can have an extremely disruptive effect on an ecosystem—natural events and human activity. Natural events, such as a volcanic eruption, a flood, or a change in the climate, can change or destroy the habitat. The local species may be driven to look for a new home or killed because they can't escape. These events are usually catastrophic to the whole ecosystem, but leave it open to be colonized by a new set of species.

VOLCANIC ERUPTION

Natural disasters...

HURRICANE

HOLDING THE KEY

An ecosystem can often cope with losing one or two minor species, but there are some animals, called keystone species, that are essential to its survival. It is often a small predator that feeds on an herbivore which, in turn, eats the main plant in the environment. Without the predator the herbivore population grows out of control and crowds out other species.

Sea otters were once plentiful off the coast of California, but were hunted almost to extinction for their fur. Without the otters, the number of sea urchins, their favorite food, exploded. Sea urchins eat kelp (a giant seaweed), which shelters fish and feeds other herbivores. As the kelp disappeared, the whole ecosystem began to collapse.

Ecosystems are a complex mixture of living things and their habitat, with different species interacting with each other like the pieces in a jigsaw puzzle. Usually an ecosystem has enough resources to sustain all the species, but if something changes it can *affect the balance* of the whole system.

Natural catastrophes are rare, sudden events, but the *effect of humans* is continuous and often more destructive. We humans are *taking over larger and larger areas* of the land for our own needs, *destroying* existing *habitats*. And the oceans are not safe, either.

Human intervention...

DEFORESTATION

SHAPING THE ENVIRONMENT

Some species play a key role in shaping and maintaining the environment. Prairie dogs dig burrows that provide homes for many other species, including burrowing owls and black-footed ferrets. Their tunnels help break up the soil and trap rainwater. They also trim the grass, removing cover for predators.

Prairie dogs are useful in their natural environment, but farmers do not like their tunnels and they have almost been wiped out in parts of the United States. This had consequences for black-footed ferrets, whose main food is prairie dogs—they almost became extinct. A breeding program has now boosted their numbers.

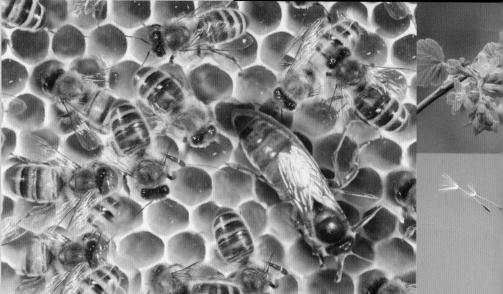
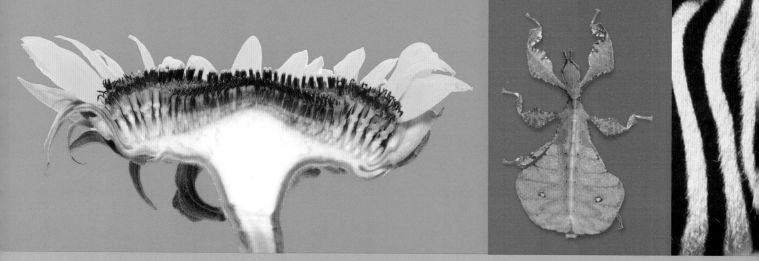

Ⓞ *Secrets of* SURVIVAL

Life isn't easy. As a *living thing* you have to find food, a mate, somewhere to take shelter, and *make sure your offspring survive*. You may need to fight, cooperate with other species, or find another way to get around problems. Or you could make yourself look better or fiercer than your rivals, *develop some weapons*, or use sneaky tricks to *disguise yourself*. Strategy and tactics will help you to survive.

HOME *sweet* HOME

BALD EAGLE

Penthouse views

Nests are built by birds to lay their eggs in. They vary from little more than a few thrown-together twigs to elaborately woven structures. The smallest, no bigger than half a walnut shell, are made by hummingbirds. The largest are built by bald eagles, who add new twigs every year until the nest weighs more than a ton. Sociable weaver birds make nests that can house up to 300 birds.

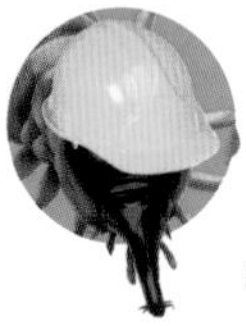

Warm air rises through chimneys

UNDER CONSTRUCTION

Designer apartments

Social insects, such as termites and bees, often live together in large colonies. Certain species of termite mix mud and saliva to build huge structures that have many chambers and even air conditioning to provide a steady flow of air through the tower. Bees and wasps build nests out of wax, mud, or chewed wood in a cavity or even under a large leaf in the tropics. They then build thousands of hexagonal cells to hold their eggs.

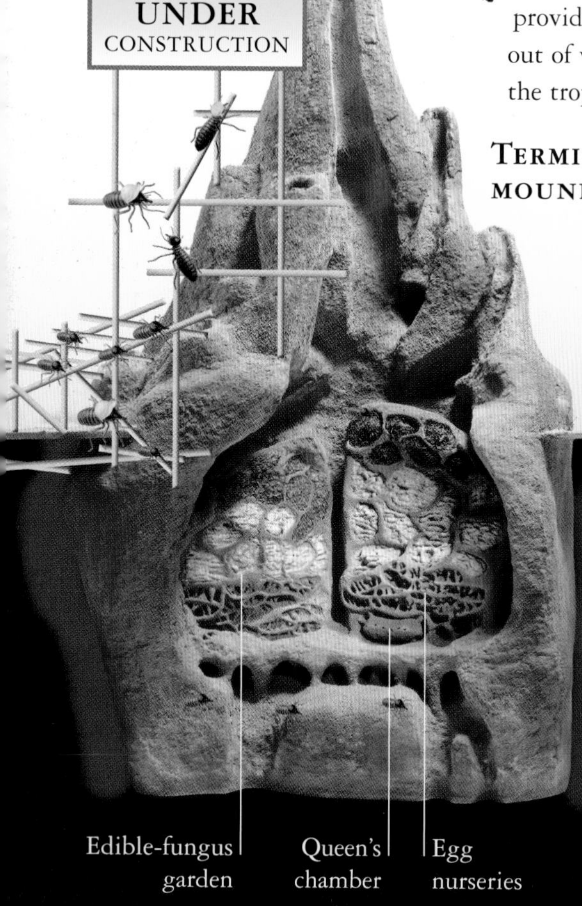

TERMITE MOUND

Underground abode

Burrows are used by many animals for shelter from the weather, but others sleep and breed there, only coming out to look for food or to find a mate. Some, such as moles or worms, spend their whole lives below ground. Empty burrows also provide a ready-made home for non-diggers.

Edible-fungus garden   Queen's chamber   Egg nurseries

Orangutans and *monkeys* make a *small nest of*

Many animals need a place for shelter. There are various reasons why they do this: somewhere to *sleep, raise their young,* escape from predators, or simply *take refuge* from the weather. Animals take advantage of natural holes in trees or rocks, but some go to great lengths to create the perfect home.

> Hey there, how are you doing with that extension?

HORNBILL

High-rise hangout

A hole high in a tree trunk is an excellent place to raise a family, which makes it an ideal home for birds and many tree-climbing animals. That doesn't always make it safe—snakes will climb trees in search of prey. Tree holes happen naturally when part of the trunk decays, or they are excavated by birds like the woodpecker. Holes at the base of the tree are used as dens by bears for shelter and to give birth to cubs. Hollow logs also provide homes for small animals and a wide variety of insect species.

UNUSUAL HOMES

Honduran white bats build a tent out of a large leaf by biting through the leaf ribs and folding it over themselves.

Female polar bears make dens in the ice during the Arctic winter to give birth and raise their cubs in safety.

Trap-door spiders dig a hole, which they seal with a lid. At night they lift the lid, grab a passing insect, and slam it shut again.

Secluded property

Caves are ideal places for animals to escape the weather. Bears occupy them during the winter and tigers use them to shelter from the heat. Fish slip into underwater caves and crevices in rocks to escape predators or to lie in wait for prey to pass by. Some marine animals use caves to protect their eggs or young. Bats use the darkness of caves to hide from daylight, only coming out at night to feed.

> I thought you said that cave was empty?

leaves and *branches* every night to sleep in.

Defending *your turf*

WARNING SIGNS
The risks involved in fighting can be costly for an animal, so most try a variety of tactics first to ward off their enemies.

WHY FIGHT?
There are a number of reasons why animals fight: to defend their territory, to get a share of any food, to gain access to mates, or to protect their young. Fighting is dangerous and can lead to injury or even death. But it does have an evolutionary benefit—the strongest survive to pass their genes on to future generations.

Making the call
Territory is often declared using calls. Birds have key perches from which they send out loud, noisy songs that tell others to keep off their turf. In the rainforest, troops of monkeys and gibbons call out to other teams that might be in the area to make sure they stay away from their trees.

STAY AWAY!

HOWLER MONKEY

What's that smell?
Scent marking is another way that animals announce their presence. Many animals have glands on the body that produce a strong odor. By rubbing against trees and bushes they leave their smell behind. Urine and droppings are also used to mark boundaries. Smells act as warnings to their own species and to others—it pays to know if a predator is around.

DUNG

INTO BATTLE
There comes a point where you have to engage the enemy. Even then it is rarely a fight to the death. Instead there may be a few tentative charges as the opponents assess each other's strengths. Most fights involve biting, kicking, and wrestling. They usually end when the weaker animal realizes that it hasn't got a chance of winning and signals that it is giving up.

Fighting is an important part of animal life. They don't do it because they enjoy being *aggressive,* but to *ensure* the *survival* of themselves and their *offspring.*

DON'T COME ANY CLOSER

If a rival strays onto your turf, it's still worth avoiding a fight if you can, so it helps to have a few tricks available to scare off the opposition.

Stand up for yourself

Making yourself look bigger than your opponent is a useful tactic. Rearing up on your hindlegs makes you look taller, while turning sideways makes you look wider. If, like a crab or scorpion, you've got a huge pair of pincers to wave, even better!

MOON BEAR

FRILLED LIZARD

Huff and puff

Puffing yourself up is another way to look larger than your rival. Birds fluff out their feathers and spread their wings or raise a crest if they have one. Some chameleons and reptiles inflate themselves with air, while elephants stick their ears out and trumpet loudly.

Spit it out

Spitting isn't usually dangerous, but it can be unpleasant. Llamas are experts at hitting their target with partly chewed food. Fulmars (seabirds) go one step further and eject smelly vomit. Worst of all, cobras spit venom into an attacker's eyes.

LLAMA

Show your teeth

Snarling, growling, and hissing are other ways to get the message across. Dogs and cats use this tactic, while pigs grind their teeth. Crocodiles spread their jaws wide open to display their formidable dentistry. Birds, too, open their beaks wide. Or you can simply stick your tongue out like the blue-tongued skink.

CROCODILE

SNAP! SNAP! SNAP!

Part of the GANG

Ever noticed how some animals are found in a crowd? From herds of wildebeest to flocks of geese and schools of fish, some species stick together. Although it may get a bit overcrowded at times, there are advantages to being part of the gang.

WHO'S IN AND WHO'S OUT

The makeup of a group can vary between species. In some there may be a mix of males and females of different ages, or all may be of a similar age or all the same sex. In many species juveniles leave to join another group or form a new one. Female elephants, however, stay in the same group all their lives, passing on their knowledge and experience.

Safety in numbers

Life as a solitary wildebeest would be too dangerous. You immediately become a target for any lion looking for lunch. Mingle with 99 other wildebeest, and the odds of you being singled out for attack drop from 100 to 1 percent. There are also 99 other pairs of eyes looking out for predators and good places to graze. The downside is that there may not be enough food for everyone, so you have to keep moving on.

I'M THE TOP BANANA!

I do wish she'd keep up with the herd.

HERD OF WILDEBEEST

Going to war

When it comes to battling to gain space or resources, then the more warriors you have available, the better. Swarms containing thousands of pavement ants fight for territory for hours at a time, biting and wrestling their rivals. Only a few are actually killed, but the skirmishes may continue for weeks until one of the groups comes out on top and claims the territory.

SWARM OF ANTS

Bringing up the kids

It's natural for parents to care for their offspring, but sometimes other members of the community pitch in to feed or babysit the young. In an extended family group there is often a dominant breeding pair and only they will have babies. By caring for their siblings, juveniles help keep the babies safe while the parents hunt, and also teach their younger brothers and sisters essential survival skills.

> HOW COME I ALWAYS END UP BABYSITTING?

COMMUNITY OF CHIMPANZEES

ON THE HUNT

Hunting in packs enables animals to catch prey that would be tricky to bring down alone. Attacks are carefully coordinated, each animal playing its part in stalking and cornering the victim. However, once the prey is caught, hierarchy takes over, with the pack leader getting the pick of the prime morsels from the carcass.

Caring and sharing

Being part of a group means that there is always someone to help get rid of those pesky parasites in difficult-to-reach places or to snuggle up to on chilly nights. But close proximity makes it easy for parasite numbers to soar out of control and disease can spread quickly. On the upside, many paws make light work when it comes to constructing homes.

AFRICAN WILD DOGS

GANG OF MEERKATS

> Follow me, ladies…

Pecking order

Not all animals in a group are equal. Most communities have a number of dominant animals at the top who get first pick of the available food, shelter, and mates. Those lower down the ranks have to make do with whatever they can beg, steal, or sneakily get away with. Keeping your position means forming alliances or being prepared to fight. Once an order is established the aggression stops.

Life in the COLONY

LIVING IN LARGE GROUPS can have advantages, but to live with thousands or even *millions of your own species* requires a special set of rules. Many insect species live and work together in order to survive. Welcome to life in a colony.

Most colonies have the same structure: at the top is a *single female*, usually called the *queen*. The lower orders are made up of mainly female *workers* and *soldiers*. The members of the colony are usually closely related. Only the queen will breed; the workers are sterile. There are a *few males* in the colony *to mate* with the queen.

Some *ant colonies* have *survived* for *hundreds of years.*

SUPERORGANISMS

Animals that live together year round in a colony are highly organized and have a strict hierarchy. Each individual is like a cell within a larger creature. Animals that live like this are described as eusocial organisms. Operating as one "superorganism" has certain advantages. By spreading out the responsibilities of life—building a home, fighting off enemies, and looking for a mate—the colony can grow large and survive for decades.

Ant army

Leafcutter ants live in impressively large colonies, sometimes numbering millions of individuals. Each colony consists of a long-lived queen attended by female workers who raise the queen's young. There are different ranks of workers who have particular jobs—chewing up leaves brought back by scouting parties, tending the fungus they cultivate on the chewed leaves, and harvesting the fungus and feeding it to the larvae. The whole nest is guarded by a troop of soldiers, who are much larger than the workers and have powerful jaws to bite through intruders.

Younger workers *clean the hive* and feed the larvae.

Larvae fed solely on *royal jelly* will develop into a *queen bee.*

The QUEEN is surrounded by *workers* who meet her *every need.*

Older workers go out to *collect pollen* and *nectar.*

Workers perform a special "waggle dance" to *communicate* to each other where a food source can be found.

Queen bee

In a honeybee colony, the queen will mate with various males to ensure a good mix of genes. Over the next few years she will lay up to 2,000 eggs a day—that's more than her own body weight! Some eggs are fertilized and go on to become female workers, and some are unfertilized and become male drones.

Mole rats

The only vertebrates that live in this type of colony are two species of mole rats. Their colonies are not as big as insect colonies and have a more equal mix of males and females. The mole rats vary in size with the smallest ones doing most of the hard labor. By the time they reach full size they do no work but are responsible for guarding the nest, defending it to the death if necessary.

They work in a production line, kicking dirt along and out to the surface.

The smallest are the hardest workers, digging and cleaning tunnels.

Phew, this is hard work—I can't wait to grow up and get some rest!

As they get older and bigger they work less hard, spending more time lounging in the central nest chamber.

Only the queen breeds, handing over the pups to the workers to raise. She spends most of her time patrolling the tunnels, checking on the workers.

GOING IT ALONE

Sexual reproduction is not the only way to increase the species. Animals such as jewel anemones and flatworms can reproduce simply by splitting in two.

New anemone

Single

JEWEL ANEMONE SPLITTING

Starts to split

Other anemones and hydras (small water creatures) use budding, in which a new animal starts to grow as part of its mother before detaching.

HYDRA BUDDING

Parthenogenesis is another method used, particularly by aphids. Here the eggs develop without the need for fertilization by sperm. The offspring are all female, identical to their parent, and are called clones. Cloning is a useful way to increase the population quickly when conditions are good and can support extra offspring. It was thought that female Komodo dragons also do this, however recent research suggests that they actually store sperm for many months after mating.

KOMODO DRAGON

When I grow up I want to be *just like you,* Mom.

The NEED

Adapt and survive

One of the biggest challenges to survival is ensuring that each generation is equipped to cope with changing conditions in their environment. To do this, animals need to produce as many offspring as they can that are different from their parents and from each other so that new features can emerge over time. Animals produce young by sexual reproduction. Special cells called eggs and sperm mix DNA from a male and a female (see p.15). That way, different variations of DNA are passed on to the young, which helps the population survive if conditions change.

Finding a mate

If you live in a large group of your own species all year round then it's not hard to find a mate, but more solitary animals or those that can't move have to find another way to produce their offspring.

 Advertising—you can do this by calling, laying a scent trail, or putting on a visual display. The downside is that it may also attract unwanted attention from predators and parasites.

 Lekking—the animal equivalent of going to a nightclub. Some animals, such as capercaillies or gemboks, gather at a regular breeding site where the males fight over the best spot to show off their dance moves. The females watch and rate their appearance and ability before pairing off.

 Find a soul mate—many solitary animals, such as albatrosses and swans pair up for life. Even though they spend most of the year apart, they meet up again in the breeding season to mate. Pairs that do this become more successful at raising young as the years go by.

If an animal is to pass on *advantageous genes* it must survive long enough to BREED. If successful, this results in individuals that are better adapted to their environment. Breeding usually involves *finding a mate* and RAISING YOUNG until they can fend for themselves. *But not all animals do it this way.*

RABBITS mature fast and breed quickly completing their life cycle rapidly.

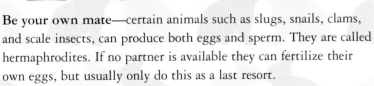

to BREED

Be your own mate—certain animals such as slugs, snails, clams, and scale insects, can produce both eggs and sperm. They are called hermaphrodites. If no partner is available they can fertilize their own eggs, but usually only do this as a last resort.

Change sides—some animals change their sex at a certain stage in their life or if conditions threaten survival of the group. This mainly happens among fish, frogs, and other hermaphrodite animals.

Synchronized spawning—hard corals synchronize their reproductive activity so that neighboring colonies release their eggs and sperm into the water at the same time. The currents mix them up, then carry the fertilized eggs away to form new colonies. Some fish do the same, coming together in huge shoals to release their eggs and sperm.

BRINGING UP BABY

When it comes to producing babies animals have two strategies—they either have a lot or just a few. Animals that don't raise their young tend to have many offspring to allow for the fact that not very many will live to become adults and reproduce.

Female frogs produce a lot of eggs in a jelly mass called frog spawn. These are fertilized by the male and grow into tadpoles and, unless they get eaten, turn into frogs.

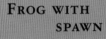

999 eggs— **HOPEFULLY** *some will survive without my help.*

FROG WITH SPAWN

The amount of time that animals spend caring for their young depends on how quickly they reach a stage where they can take care of themselves. Large-brained social animals such as humans and elephants tend to give birth to single offspring, because their babies need time to grow and learn.

HUMANS

DRESS for

Animals come in many colors. Some are drab, some are patterned, and some are every color of the rainbow. But there are many reasons why animals have evolved such a variety of colors...

It all comes down to one thing—*survival of the species.*

ONE OF THE GANG

Color helps animals recognize others of the same species. Not all animals can see in color—some see only patterns of light and shade. Others can see all or parts of the visible spectrum and sometimes infrared or ultraviolet. Animals with the best color vision are often very colorful themselves.

> NOW YOU SEE ME...

> ... NOW YOU DON'T

> *Hey, where did my lunch go?*

Blend in

The ability to blend into the background is a distinct advantage. For predators, being able to able to sneak up on your prey without being seen means you are much more likely to get your dinner. For prey animals, being hard to see ensures you don't become the target.

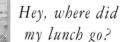

Spots and stripes are used by animals that live in forests or long grass to help break up the outline of the animal.

Lions only see in shades of gray.

One of the best ways to *hide* yourself is to look like *something else,*

Stick or...

STICK INSECT

... leaf or...

... thorn or...

LEAF INSECT

THORN BUG

Disguising yourself to look like something else is called mimicry. Many animals have evolved to look like dead leaves, twigs, seaweed, or even bird droppings. Predators are fooled into thinking it's not something they're interested in or that it's something they should avoid. Birds won't eat hoverflies because they look like wasps, which will sting if eaten. However, the flower mantis not only uses its appearance to hide, but also to attract its insect prey. Plants use mimicry too.

Look, but don't touch

If you want to stay hidden then drab colors, such as browns and grays, are your best option. However, if you want to be noticed, the brighter you are, the better. Species that are poisonous or taste bad have striking colors that act as a warning. Red, white, yellow, and black usually mean "don't come near me."

Distraction

Bright colors are also used as a distraction. Some butterflies and coral reef fish have circles of color on their wings or at the rear end of their body that look like eyes. Predators think they are attacking the head, which gives the animal a chance to get away without suffering too much damage.

CHANGE OF COLOR

Some animals are capable of changing color. Arctic hares (pictured) do this seasonally, swapping their dull summer coloring for pure white in the winter so they are hidden against the snow. Others, such as squid and chameleons, can change at will, using color to show their mood or to court a mate. Many lizards change to help them absorb or lose heat.

SUMMER

WINTER

these are the MASTERS OF DISGUISE...

... *flower* or...

... *bee* or...

FLOWER MANTIS

BEE ORCHID

The bee orchid has flowers that look like a female bee, which attracts male bees. The male tries to mate with the "female," fertilizing the flower in the process.

HOVERFLY

FLASHY DRESSERS

Color is used by many species to attract rather than repel. In many cases it is the male that is the gaudier—females are usually dull by comparison.

PEACOCK

PEAHEN

The main purpose is to attract a mate, so the brighter, the better. Those that are strongest and healthiest tend to have the best coloration and methods of displaying it, so they will attract more females. Female peafowl (peahens) are attracted to male birds that have more "eyes" on their tails than their rivals.

As well as color, other impressive attributes—such as a large set of antlers— can attract a mate.

RED DEER STAG

71

Deadly WEAPONS

A quick bite

Poison is the ultimate defensive weapon for an animal under attack, but in most cases it is used to kill or subdue prey. Spiders and snakes deliver their venom by biting. Snakes have hollow fangs that allow the venom to flow from a gland in their upper jaw into their victim.

My venomous sting protects me from hungry predators—and it also kills my prey.

SCORPION

RATTLESNAKE

WASP

ELECTRIC EEL

Truly shocking

Some fish use shock tactics to stun prey and deter predators. Torpedo rays, stargazers, and electric eels have cells that produce an electric discharge. They usually use this to sense the environment around them, but can also unleash it to deadly effect—an electric eel can deliver up to 650 volts.

OUCH!

LIONFISH

PORCUPINE

SEA SLUG

Disgusting dinners

Many invertebrates, reptiles, and amphibians exude horrible-tasting, and sometimes poisonous, substances through their skin or from glands on the body. Most are brightly colored to warn predators that eating them is a bad idea. Some frogs and birds "borrow" poison by eating toxic beetles.

PISTOL SHRIMP

Get your claws out

Sharp claws that can slash an opponent deters them from coming too close. Pincers, as found on lobsters, scorpions, and crabs, are a type of hinged claw that can be snapped shut with great force. Pistol shrimp have an oversized claw that closes so fast it causes a bubble to form, creating a shock wave in the water capable of stunning both predators and prey.

Don't come near us—we're dangerous!

Every animal or plant is a potential dinner for another organism. But rather than surrendering to a grisly fate, many have developed weapons to fight back against a predator. These impressively dangerous spiky, sharp, or poisonous weapons are also used to catch food.

WIDOW SPIDER

BEWARE—I'M SMALL BUT DEADLY!

OTHER OFFENSIVE WEAPONS

Tarantulas can flick the hairs on their abdomen at opponents. The hairs are barbed and can irritate bare skin.

Sting in the tail

Stings are another way to inject venom. They are usually found in the tails of scorpions and insects, such as bees and wasps, and are used to deter bigger animals or to kill smaller ones for food. Soft-bodied underwater animals also use stinging tentacles to zap anything that gets too close.

STARGAZER

TORPEDO RAY

Skunks and stink badgers have glands at the base of the tail that contain a foul-smelling liquid which they can squirt up to 13 ft (4 m) quite accurately.

A prickly subject

Spikes and thorns are an effective deterrent against anything trying to wrap its jaws around you. Porcupines have stiff, hollow spines that they raise when threatened. In some fish, such as the lionfish or weever fish, the spines also deliver poison.

Boxer crabs often encourage stinging sea anemones to grow on their claws so they can wave them at enemies.

SPANISH FESTOON BUTTERFLY

I'm not as tasty as I look!

CRAB

The **Texas horned lizard** squirts blood from a gland near the corner of its eye. The blood contains a foul-tasting chemical that repels all attackers.

Taking advantage

There are some living things that just can't help taking advantage of others. They often get away with it, but crime doesn't always pay…

Six victims speak out about the shocking

I didn't know he was living there, but I had a STRANGE FEELING that I was eating for two.

VICTIM
Cow

CRIMINAL
Tapeworm

I'd only gone out for a few hours but when I came back HE'D MOVED IN and wouldn't leave.

VICTIM
Gopher tortoise

CRIMINAL
Burrowing owl

That penguin STOLE THE FOOD right out of my mouth—and in broad daylight, too!

VICTIM
Pelican

CRIMINAL
Galápagos penguin

PARASITES

Parasites are plants or animals that live in or on another species. They feed directly from them, absorbing nutrients that they wouldn't be able to obtain or make for themselves. Some parasites target only a single species. Others have a complex life cycle where they change hosts as they move from eggs and larvae to adults. Tapeworms live in the guts of animals, feeding on partly digested food. They also live in humans.

SQUATTERS

It takes a lot of effort to build the perfect home so if you can find one that's ready to move into, all the better. Burrowing animals, such as aardvarks or prairie dogs may take days to dig out tunnels underground. If they leave for any length of time an opportunist may sneak in and take it over. Burrowing owls are capable of building their own burrows but will take advantage of a gopher tortoise's excavations if they can.

THIEVES AND MUGGERS

Why spend hours searching for food when you can steal it from someone else? Many animals take advantage of their size, strength, or sheer cunning to make another give up its dinner. Some will even rob members of their own species. Galápagos penguins often chase pelicans and force them to open their beaks rather than hunt for their own fish. However, they risk injury if their victim objects.

Getting another species to do all the hard work needed to support your lifestyle is a good survival strategy. **The secret is not to overdo it.**

CRIMINAL Mistletoe

VICTIM Tree

Plants do it too... Mistletoe is a parasitic plant that lives on other trees. It has special roots that push into cracks in the bark and penetrate the wood so that it can draw water and nutrients into its own stems.

offences committed against them:

IT WAS AS IF I'D BEEN TAKEN OVER. They were controlling my mind. How horrible is THAT?

VICTIM Caterpillar

CRIMINAL Voodoo wasp

I thought he was my friend, and then he turned on me and MADE ME HIS SLAVE.

VICTIM Ant

CRIMINAL Slavemaker ant

Scratch, scratch, scratch—the itching drove me crazy. THEY DIDN'T EVEN ASK me if they could hitch a ride.

VICTIM Dog

CRIMINAL Flea

USURPERS AND BODYSNATCHERS

Bringing up young is hard work so some species have found the perfect solution—get someone else to do it. Certain insects and birds lay their eggs in the nests of other species and get their hosts to raise the offspring with their own. Voodoo wasps are more sinister—they inject their eggs into a caterpillar. The larvae release a chemical that controls the caterpillar's brain and makes it take care of them.

SLAVERS AND TYRANTS

Several species of ant make slaves of other ants by invading their colony and taking it over, or by their stealing eggs to bring up as servants. The enslaved ants are made to tend to the queen and her eggs, search for food, and defend the colony against attack because the invaders can't do it for themselves. Slaves will even carry their masters to a new colony. The captive ants get their own back by killing the larvae of their oppressors.

HITCHHIKERS

Hitching a ride on another animal means you don't have to expend energy to find a new source of food. Ticks, lice, and fleas hop onto a passing animal and either suck its blood or use it as transportation to a new host. Fish that are poor swimmers, like the remora, have a sucker to attach themselves to larger fish. Comb jellies are often infested with amphipods (tiny crustaceans) that burrow into their host.

the Long Walk

There are many reasons why animals migrate. Some do it regularly at certain times of the year. Others do it because their environment has changed and they rarely come back. Not all members of a population migrate—in many cases only those of breeding age go on the move.

Overcrowding

When a population gets too big for the available space or food supply, some have to move away. Locusts and Norway lemmings often form breakaway groups when it all gets too crowded.

I don't know why they're all following me—I have no idea where I'm going!

Finding a mate

Animals that live solitary lives often migrate to find a mate and breed. For two or three weeks a year, millions of red crabs on Christmas Island make their way from their rain forest burrows and walk down to the beach to mate and lay their eggs in the water.

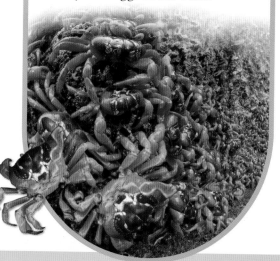

Knowing the way

Some animals travel thousands of miles when they migrate, but many will never have traveled the route before. So how do they know where to go? Animals that make the journey alone inherit this knowledge from their parents. Others, such as geese and swallows, travel together. They navigate using landmarks and the position of the Sun, Moon, and stars. Some birds have an internal compass that picks up Earth's magnetic field.

Nomads

For some animals, wandering from place to place is a way of life. Grazing animals, such as vicuñas, guanacos (pictured), and zebras, are constantly on the move to find new pasture. They don't always travel the same route, they simply go where the grass is.

Arctic terns make a **44,000 mile (71,000 km)** round

The sight of *thousands of animals* moving across a landscape is one of the wonders of the world. But why do they do it? It's not for a change of scenery—many are driven by a biological need to find food, water, or mates. This type of annual movement is called *migration*.

Many migrating animals travel long distances to reach their *feeding* or *breeding* grounds. Most travel the same route there and back, *some without stopping.*

ONE-WAY TICKET

American monarch butterflies head south to Mexico to spend the winter. As they start the return trip, they mate and die. The next generation continues the journey, but it is often the third or even fourth generation that finally makes it home.

Salmon spend their adult lives out at sea, but when they reach breeding age they journey back to the freshwater streams where they hatched to lay their own eggs. Exhausted by the effort, they die after spawning.

Getting ready

Long-distance travelers have to be in peak condition before setting off. Many species don't stop along the way for food and water, so they have to build up reserves of fat to provide them with energy.

Time to go

While some animals only move when they are forced to, others have a built-in instinct for when it is time to set off. Changes in day length or seasonal weather conditions can affect food supplies or make it too hot, cold, wet, or dry for the animal. If the animal can't adapt to the changes, for example, by growing a thicker coat or hibernating, it has to migrate.

Giving birth

Animals do their best to protect their young, so many migrate to places that offer shelter or the chance to raise their offspring away from predators. Emperor penguins walk many miles into Antarctica and endure harsh conditions to bring up their chicks safely.

Changing seasons

Most migrations are seasonal and occur because the lack of food or water makes it impossible for the animal to stay in one place. Those that move to find food include geese, reindeer, and whales. Humpback whales make some of the longest journeys. Their feeding grounds are not the best place to breed, so they move from the poles to warmer waters to have their calves.

trip from *pole to pole* every year.

Life beneath *the* waves

Oceans cover nearly 70 percent of this planet, making them the largest of all habitats. There are plenty of creatures living beneath the waves, but life here presents a very different set of challenges to living on the land.

Seawater contains 35 parts of dissolved salts for every 1,000 parts of water.

IT'S SALTY DOWN HERE!

It's too salty

Even though the salt in seawater is heavily diluted, it would damage any land animal or plant that tried to drink it. However, the water inside the bodies of marine organisms is as salty as the water around them, which keeps them in balance. Fish drink seawater but they secrete excess salt through their gills. Mammals rarely drink seawater and obtain most of the water they need from their food. They get rid of the salt in their urine.

SEAL

Keeping warm

The surface layers of the ocean can be very warm, especially near the coast where the water is shallower. In the deep water and around the poles it is extremely cold. Most marine life is cold-blooded, matching the temperature of the water around it. Sometimes, however, that is too cold—there are fish living in polar waters that have a type of antifreeze in their blood to keep it flowing.

ANTARCTIC TOOTHFISH

Warm-blooded animals face a more severe challenge. Most have an insulating layer of fat around the body called blubber, which also serves as an energy store. Sea otters have thick fur that traps a layer of air next to their skin so that it never gets wet. Marine mammals can also control their blood flow: since the blood vessels are close together, cold blood returning from the extremities to the body core is warmed by blood flowing back out to the limbs.

ANGLER FISH

Swimming in the dark

Sunlight cannot penetrate more than about a yard through water, so organisms that rely on photosynthesis, such as corals and seaweed, are found in shallow water. It gets much darker as you go deeper. It is hard to see down here, so animals rely on other senses—smell, echolocation, hearing, and changes in water pressure—to detect food and enemies. Some animals produce their own light— called bioluminescence—to attract prey or mates.

COMB JELLYFISH

Seabirds have tiny glands in the nasal cavity that collect the salt, which they then shake or sneeze out.

Just try getting me off this rock!

BREATHING

Like land animals, marine creatures breathe oxygen. Mammals and reptiles have lungs, so they have to come to the surface at intervals to take a gulp of air. They are good at holding their breath and diverting blood away from nonessential areas, such as the flippers, so that more oxygen goes to the heart and brain.

However, most underwater creatures have to get oxygen from the water rather than the air. Fish and invertebrates that spend all their time submerged have gills or respire through their skin to extract oxygen from water flowing over them.

Gills
Water

Fish have gills on either side of their head. Blood vessels here filter out the oxygen from seawater.

Mouth

Rocky shores

Organisms that live close to the shore may not have to cope with pressure or lack of light, but they do have other challenges. Invertebrates and plants are constantly pounded by waves and they have to anchor themselves securely to a rock. Other animals are left exposed when the tide goes out, and have a protective shell that they can seal to prevent themselves drying out.

For every 33 ft (10 m) below the surface, the *pressure* INCREASES by the equivalent of one atmosphere.

HELP!

They say there's a lot of pressure on those who live down here…

… *but since we don't have lungs, it doesn't bother us at all.*

Under pressure

Although we can't feel it, on dry land we have the weight of the atmosphere pressing down on every square inch of our bodies. Dive into the ocean and you also have the weight of the water pressing down. The deeper you go, the more the pressure increases and squashes the airspaces of animals with lungs. Instead of resisting the pressure, deep divers such as sperm whales and elephant seals can collapse their lungs, slow their heartbeat, and store oxygen in their muscles. This also helps them to sink, so they don't spend as much energy swimming. If human scuba divers return to the surface too quickly they can die from the rapid change in pressure, which causes bubbles to form in the blood

Scattering the SEED

Plants can't move around to find a mate or more room to grow, so they have evolved ingenious ways to make new plants and spread themselves around. Some produce mini versions of themselves that stay close to the original plant. Others make seeds that can be carried by wind, water, or animals and dispersed over a wide area.

INSIDE A FLOWER

Most flowering plants reproduce by producing seeds. The flower contains the reproductive organs, which include the stigma, ovary, and anthers. The anthers contain pollen, which is transferred to the stigma of another flower during pollination. Cells from the pollen travel down to the ovary, which contains the eggs. The pollen fertilizes the eggs and they develop into seeds.

INSIDE A SUNFLOWER

Pollen

Anther

Ovary

Seed

How plants are pollinated

In order for pollination to take place, pollen needs to be transferred from one flower to another (or between male and female parts of the same flower). There are many different ways in which pollen is transported. Pollen is very light so many plants rely on the wind to carry it to another plant. Others attract insects, animals, and birds using a sweet, sugary liquid called nectar. The pollen sticks to them and rubs off when they visit another flower.

Spreading spores

Plants that don't have flowers, such as mosses, ferns, and worts, reproduce using spores. Unlike seeds, spores don't have much food stored so they are only released when conditions are right for a quick germination. Large numbers of spores are produced in the hope that a few will survive.

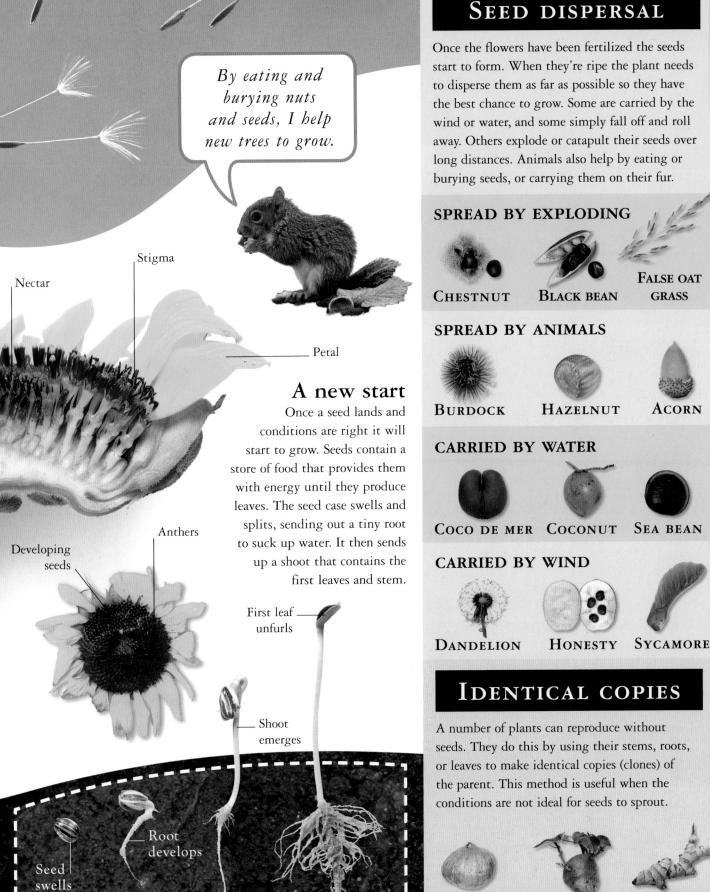

By eating and burying nuts and seeds, I help new trees to grow.

Nectar

Stigma

Petal

A new start

Once a seed lands and conditions are right it will start to grow. Seeds contain a store of food that provides them with energy until they produce leaves. The seed case swells and splits, sending out a tiny root to suck up water. It then sends up a shoot that contains the first leaves and stem.

Developing seeds

Anthers

First leaf unfurls

Shoot emerges

Root develops

Seed swells

SEED DISPERSAL

Once the flowers have been fertilized the seeds start to form. When they're ripe the plant needs to disperse them as far as possible so they have the best chance to grow. Some are carried by the wind or water, and some simply fall off and roll away. Others explode or catapult their seeds over long distances. Animals also help by eating or burying seeds, or carrying them on their fur.

SPREAD BY EXPLODING

CHESTNUT   BLACK BEAN   FALSE OAT GRASS

SPREAD BY ANIMALS

BURDOCK   HAZELNUT   ACORN

CARRIED BY WATER

COCO DE MER   COCONUT   SEA BEAN

CARRIED BY WIND

DANDELION   HONESTY   SYCAMORE

IDENTICAL COPIES

A number of plants can reproduce without seeds. They do this by using their stems, roots, or leaves to make identical copies (clones) of the parent. This method is useful when the conditions are not ideal for seeds to sprout.

BULB   TUBER   RHIZOME

The ULTIMATE animal?

HUMANS are **just like** any other *animal*—we all need oxygen to *breathe*, *water* to drink, and *food* to provide energy. However, over thousands of years humans have evolved a unique set of skills and abilities that enable us to overcome some of the many difficulties that every organism faces in the struggle to survive.

Brain power

One of our greatest assets is the human brain, which is large for our body size and highly developed. Unlike many other animals we are self-aware, can solve problems, have language, and can make tools. We are not alone in these abilities—apes, elephants, and dolphins can all recognize themselves in mirrors, use tools, and communicate. Like us, these animals have spindle neurons (very large brain cells) that allow rapid communication across the brain. These play a key role in the development of intelligent behavior.

Social intelligence

Humans are not necessarily cleverer than other organisms. What we do possess is the ability to create and learn and turn that into a cultural knowledge that we share with others. When you play with your friends and go to school you are acquiring this knowledge and culture. If only one human knew everything, humans would not last long as a species. Dolphins, chimps, and elephants also pass on skills such as making and using tools to catch food, which suggests that they too have a simple form of culture.

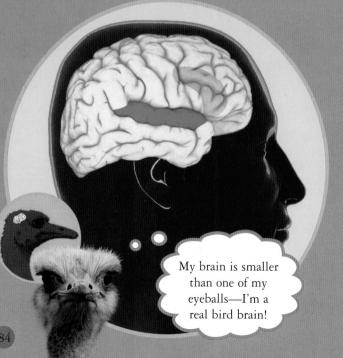

My brain is smaller than one of my eyeballs—I'm a real bird brain!

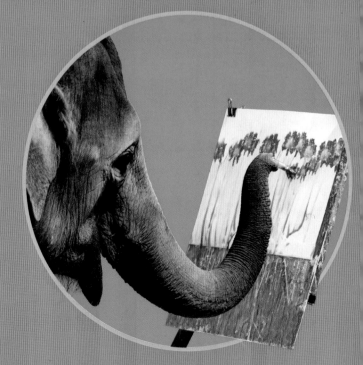

There is one species that has *taken over the whole planet—**humans.*** From *pole to pole*, humans have found a way to live and survive in every environment. This has put us in direct competition with **every other organism** for food, space, and other natural resources.

APE MAN

Humans are primates and, more specifically, members of a group of animals called hominids, or great apes. This group includes chimpanzees, orangutans, and gorillas. Our closest relatives are chimpanzees, who share 98.7 percent of our DNA. Scientists think our last common ancestor lived about 7 million years ago. Since then, there have been many species of humans but we, *Homo sapiens*, are the only one left.

Fitter and faster

Humans are also capable of making themselves physically better than average. Think of athletes competing in the Olympics. They train hard so that they can run, jump, and swim faster than ordinary humans. No other animal does that, because if they spent their time training they might not be able to escape from unexpected predators or run after their food at a moment's notice. Other animals only have to be fit enough to survive in the wild, and they don't waste their energy unnecessarily.

It's good to talk

Other animals make calls that indicate certain things, such as alarm, warning, or location. Humans, too, began to communicate with grunts and hand signals. Later, single words were joined together into sentences so that ideas could be expressed. By rearranging individual words humans can create endless new messages. Scientists have found that birds and dolphins have regional accents. There is even evidence that members of a dolphin pod give each other names so that they can talk directly to one another.

Hello there, where have you come from? You're not a member of my pod!

What was that? I don't understand your accent!

You are *not* Alone

When you look in a mirror, you probably see just one living thing—*yourself*. But what you may not realize is that you are a WALKING ECOSYSTEM and that you *share your body* with millions of other organisms. Some are good, some are bad, and most are not nice to think about. Here's a guided tour of your fellow travelers.

Eyelashes

These stumpy-legged little mites are around $1/100$ in (0.3 mm) long and live head-down in your eyelash follicles. They spend their time eating skin cells and breeding, although they may emerge at night for a wander around your face.

Mouth

Your mouth is full of bacteria. They coat the surface of your teeth, gums, and lining of your mouth and share your food. Around 25,000 different species live there, with 1,000 of these on your teeth where they form a yellow furry film called plaque. If left to harden, plaque makes holes in your teeth.

Hair

Head lice are tiny, wingless insects that suck blood from your scalp and stick their eggs to your hair. They cause itchy bumps on your skin but are not dangerous. They can spread rapidly from person to person and are not fussy about whether your hair is clean or dirty.

Gut

Adult humans carry around 3¼ lb (1.5 kg) of bacteria in their guts. Most of these play a key part in digesting food and turning it into vital nutrients. But sometimes they can be overwhelmed by an invasion of bad bacteria and that's when you get an upset stomach.

FRIENDLY TRAVELERS

UNWANTED VISITORS

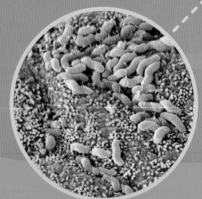

Belly button

Scientists have recently found around 1,458 new species of bacteria hiding in belly buttons. This site is a haven for bacteria because it doesn't secrete protective oils or waxes like other parts of the body, creating the perfect conditions for growth.

Skin

Every inch of your skin is covered in millions of bacteria. They feed on your sweat and produce a nasty odor when they metabolize it. Smelly as they are, they actually help your skin to stay healthy by keeping more deadly forms of bacteria at bay.

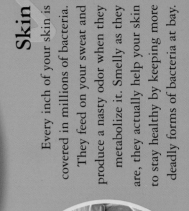

Look in a **mirror** and say hello to the **90 *trillion*** other creatures looking back at you!

Hands

Warts are caused by a virus called the human papillomavirus. They pop up in various places on your body, especially on your hands. Warts on your feet are called plantar warts.

Nerves

Some viruses lie dormant inside the body long after your symptoms have gone. The virus that causes chicken pox lingers in the nerves and can erupt years later as shingles, a painful condition that causes patches of your skin to tingle and burn.

Feet

If you wander around with bare feet at swimming pools you may pick up a parasitic fungus called athlete's foot. It thrives in the damp conditions between your toes but can spread to other areas of your body including your groin, your scalp, and under your nails.

LIFE at *the*

NOT EVERYWHERE on our planet is a nice place to live. Some places are boiling hot, others are freezing cold, extremely salty, or have no oxygen. Yet there is always some life form that manages to survive there. We call these organisms *extremophiles*.

IN HOT WATER

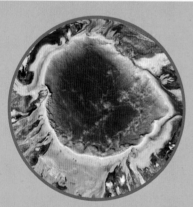

HOT SPRING

In volcanic regions, where boiling water pours out of Earth's crust through geysers and vents, temperatures reach over 104°F (40°C) and the water is often full of sulphurous compounds. Although conditions are harsh, certain bacteria seem to thrive here. The green and red colors of the Grand Prismatic Spring in Yellowstone National Park are the result of bacteria growing around the edge of the pool.

UNDER PRESSURE

RED TUBEWORM

On the deep seafloor, hydrothermal vents spew torrents of superheated, sulphur-rich water into the ocean. Temperatures inside the vents exceed 300°F (150°C) and the pressurized environment has no oxygen. Scientists have found microbes that can survive here, and not only that—the vents are also home to giant tubeworms, Pompeii worms, crabs, shrimp, and fish. They feed on the bacteria living in this poisonous environment.

FEELING CHILLY

MARINE PLANKTON

At the other end of the thermometer are organisms that live in icy conditions. These creatures have developed special proteins that act like antifreeze to prevent the fluid inside their cells turning to ice. Despite the cold, these areas of Earth are full of life. Polar waters contain bacteria that are food for larger krill, zooplankton, and fish. Some icefish are so sensitive that they would die from heatstroke if the temperature ever rose above 39°F (4°C).

EXTREMES

Most extremophiles are archaebacteria. More complex organisms may survive in hostile conditions, but only for short periods of time. What they all have in common is that they have developed mechanisms that allow them to handle the extreme environments.

A DOSE OF SALTS

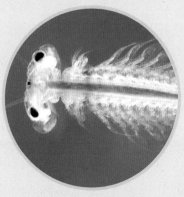

BRINE SHRIMP

Inland lakes that can't drain into the sea slowly build up very high levels of mineral salts in their waters. These salts can be acidic or alkaline substances, or simply common salt, sodium chloride. Many land organisms can't cope with salty surroundings because it draws water out of their cells and they die. However, some bacteria and algae can live in the salt, along with brine shrimp and brine flies, which are food for birds.

DRY AS DUST

LICHEN

No organism can survive without water, but some can manage with a very small amount. Fungi are the most successful at getting by on very little water, using their root-like hyphae to share moisture and nutrients. Molds are also able to spread quickly across dry foods, such as grains and nuts. Some lichens, too, can live on baking hot rocks in the desert, almost shutting down their growth until it rains. Their spores have thick coats to prevent them drying out.

REAL EXTREMISTS

COFFINFISH

Inhabitants of other extremes include **barophiles**, such as coffinfish, which live in high-pressure conditions, mainly at the bottom of the sea. **Radioresistants** can cope with levels of radiation that would kill other organisms. **Anaerobic extremophiles**, such as the bacteria that live in the guts of animals, are able to live without oxygen. **Polyextremophiles** can even survive several different extremes at once.

WEIRD *but wonderful*

I look much better in the dark!

Slime molds

If you see a jelly-like mass moving slowly across your lawn, it's probably a slime mold. Slime molds are protists. When the time's right for a cellular slime mold to reproduce, the individual slug-like cells glue themselves together to form a single mass and live as one. Some of the cells form the fruiting body, while others become spores.

Viperfish

This fearsome fish has sharp teeth like glassy needles that stick out from its jaw. In fact, they protrude so far that it has to open its jaw really wide to get food inside. The viperfish also has a devious trick to catch its prey: it has a light-emitting organ called a photophore on its top fin, which it uses to lure fish toward its jaws.

I NEED TO KEEP MY COOL—IF I GET TOO HOT, I MIGHT JUST FALL APART!

Venus flytrap

Lurking in boggy conditions is this fly-eating plant called a Venus flytrap. Its leaves are hinged into two lobes colored red to attract insects. When an insect touches the sensitive hairs inside the lobes, the plant snaps shut trapping it inside. Then enzymes get to work, digesting the prey while it's still alive.

ORGANISMS come in *all shapes* and *sizes* and have a wide variety of different lifestyles. Even so, some of them are just plain weird by anyone's standards. Here are a few of the ***bizarre*** *things* that share our planet.

Aye-aye

The aye-aye is such a spooky-looking mammal, it is regarded as a demon in its native Madagascar. This nocturnal primate uses echolocation to find its prey, tapping on trees with its long middle finger and listening for the sound of insects under the bark. Then it uses its extra-long finger to fish them out.

Axolotl

Axolotls are a type of salamander. Unlike other amphibians they never grow up and walk on land. Instead, they keep their feathery gills and spend all their lives in the water. Axolotls have a unique ability to regenerate lost limbs and even parts of their brain, which makes them interesting subjects for medical scientists.

Ice worms

Ice worms live in glaciers in the Pacific Northwest and Canada. They come out at night to feed on algae, but retreat back under the ice at dawn. If they were to warm up above 41°F (5°C) they would literally melt and fall apart. Scientists are unsure how they manage to tunnel through the ice—some think they secrete a chemical that melts the ice in front of them. They are also found in freezing-cold methane deposits at the bottom of the ocean.

Horseshoe crab

These strange-looking creatures are a type of "living fossil"—survivors of animals that lived 300 million years ago. Horseshoe crabs are sea dwellers, but are related to spiders and scorpions. The head and chest are fused together, and they have six pairs of limbs, all covered by a hard outer shell.

Out of this WORLD

AS FAR AS WE KNOW, Earth is the only planet that sustains life. However, if you think about how many stars and planets there are in the Universe, chances are that there are other living things out there. But would they be the same as the plants, animals, fungi, and bacteria we see around us? *Maybe one day we'll find out.*

IS THERE OTHER LIFE IN OUR SOLAR SYSTEM?

We have yet to detect life on the other planets and moons in our solar system. Only Earth lies in the habitable zone, but from what has recently been discovered about extremophiles (see p.88–89), scientists suspect that there could be traces of life on Mars or the moons Enceladus, Europa, Io, and Titan. We know that some bacteria can thrive in the hostile conditions found on these worlds.

ALIEN VISITORS?

For aliens to land on Earth they would have to overcome the problems of space travel. It took 3.5 billion years for life on Earth to become capable of visiting our own Moon, so any aliens would need to come from a planet where life has been around for a long time. Few planets are old or stable enough for that to have happened.

NO PLACE LIKE HOME

Out of the eight planets in our solar system, life only exists on Earth. This is because Earth lies in what is called the habitable zone. This is the distance a planet has to be from its star for water to be liquid and is the reason why there is no life on our neighbours, Venus and Mars. The planet also needs to have a hot interior and enough gravity to hold on to an atmosphere.

Too hot for life

VENUS

Habitable zone (just right for life)

EARTH

Too cold for life

MARS

LITTLE GREEN MEN

In movies, aliens are usually made to look like humans but with big almond-shaped eyes and no hair, or as strange creatures with three heads and five arms. But there is no guarantee that they will look like that. They may resemble some of the weird and wonderful things that live on Earth because certain body shapes and structures are ideal for certain environments: torpedo shapes are best for swimming, paired legs are good for walking, wings are necessary for flying, and eyes are useful for detecting light. Evolution on other planets is as likely to have produced as many strange organisms as it has on Earth.

This is no alien—it is a creature called *Opabinia* that lived on Earth 500 million years ago!

LOW GRAVITY

IN DIFFICULT CONDITIONS

If there is life on another planet it probably has to contend with different physical conditions than Earth. It may have a different gravity, day length, temperature, or atmosphere, which would have an effect on the organism's body shape, way of moving, energy needs, and life cycle. For example, life on planets with high gravity would be very low to the ground to survive the crushing pressure of the atmosphere. Imagine a world of short, squat people and plants. The opposite would happen with low gravity—plants would grow very tall and animals would have to be tall to reach them.

HIGH GRAVITY

Mars

Explorations of Mars found water ice at its poles and there may be liquid water under the surface. However, Mars has very little atmosphere and is blasted by radiation. If there is life, it probably lies beneath the surface.

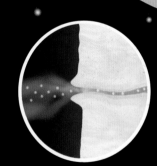

Enceladus and Europa

These two moons are thought to have liquid water under their icy surfaces. Both have hot interiors, so organisms could be living around underwater hydrothermal vents similar to those on Earth.

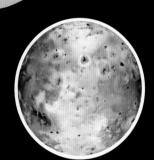

Io

This is one of the few moons with an atmosphere. It is volcanically active and has a hot inner core. There is evidence of complex chemicals, but any life would have to cope with lethal radiation from Jupiter.

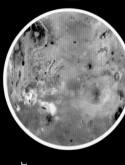

Titan

Titan has the most potential for supporting life. Its atmosphere contains amino acids that are the basis for life on Earth. The conditions are similar to those of a young Earth, although there is no liquid water.

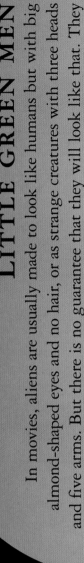

GLOSSARY

Adaptation A feature of an animal or plant that helps it to survive and reproduce in its environment.

Algae (*Singular* alga) Simple, nonflowering plants. Seaweeds are algae.

Amino acid A chemical that is used to make proteins in cells.

Amphibian A cold-blooded animal that can live on land and in water.

Arthropod An invertebrate animal that has a hard exoskeleton, a segmented body, and jointed limbs.

Biodiversity The number and variety of species living in a particular place.

Broadleaf A type of tree that has wide leaves that drop off in winter.

Cell The smallest independent part of a living thing.

Cellulose A chemical found in the walls of plant cells.

Chlorophyll The green pigment that gives plants their color.

Chloroplast A tiny organelle found in plant cells where photosynthesis occurs.

Climate The weather conditions that are usual for an area over a long period of time.

Cnidarians A group of soft-bodied animals that live in water. They include jellyfish and anemones.

Colony A group of animals living closely together or joined together in a structure.

Commensalism A relationship between two organisms where one benefits and the other is neither helped nor harmed.

Crustacean A hard-shelled animal with a pair of limbs on each body segment and two pairs of antennae.

Decomposer An organism that helps to break down dead material into essential nutrients that can be returned to the soil.

DNA (deoxyribonucleic acid) The chemical code that details everything about an organism and how it functions.

Dormancy When organisms slow or suspend their normal functions until conditions improve.

Ecosystem The plants, fungi, animals, and bacteria that live together in a particular environment.

Element A pure chemical substance that consists of a single type of atom.

Enzyme A type of protein found in a cell that is used to break or join molecules.

Evolution The process by which living things change over millions of years to become more suited to their environment.

Extinction When the last remaining organism in a species dies out leaving no offspring.

Exoskeleton A hard, external skeleton that protects an invertebrate animal's body.

Extremophile An organism that can survive under extreme physical conditions.

Fertilization The fusing together of male and female cells to produce a new organism.

Genes Sections of DNA that specify the body features and the characteristics of an organism.

Glycolysis The process used by cells to break down sugars into smaller molecules.

Habitat The place or environment where an animal lives naturally.

Hermaphrodite An animal that carries both male and female sex cells so that it can produce offspring when no mate is available.

Hibernation The ability of some animals to slow their bodily activities for a period so that they appear to be in a deep sleep. This usually happens when food is scarce.

PLANT CELL

Hydrothermal vent An opening on the seafloor that pours out hot water and chemicals from inside Earth's crust.

Hyphae The root-like structures produced by fungi and molds.

Invertebrate An animal without a backbone.

Larvae The intermediate stage that insects pass through, often as a grub or caterpillar, before they become an adult.

Mammal An animal that has fur or hair and feeds its young on milk.

Marsupial A mammal that gives birth to underdeveloped young, which it carries in a pouch.

Meiosis A method of reproduction whereby offspring have a different combination of genes from their parents.

Messenger RNA A single-stranded nucleic acid used to copy and make proteins in a cell.

Mitochondria The parts of a cell that convert food into energy.

Mitosis A method of reproduction that produces offspring that are identical to the parent.

Migrate To move from one area to another to breed or feed, usually at a set time each year.

Molecule A group of at least two atoms held together by a chemical bond.

Mutualism A relationship between two organisms from which both species benefit.

DNA MOLECULE

Nutrient A substance that is essential for the growth and maintenance of an organism.

Omnivore An animal that eats meat, plants, and fungi.

Organism A living thing.

Parasite An organism that uses another organism to help it survive, but causes harm to its host.

Parthenogenesis The method used by some animals to reproduce without the need for a mate. It results in female offspring that are identical to the mother.

Photosynthesis The process plants use to make sugars out of water, carbon dioxide, and light.

Pigment A chemical compound that gives something its color.

Pollination The process by which flowering plants transfer pollen so they can reproduce and set seed.

Population The number of any one species living in a particular place.

Predator An animal that kills and eats other animals.

Prey An animal that is hunted and killed by another for food.

Protists Microorganisms with very simple cell structures.

Reptile A cold-blooded animal with a scaly skin. Most lay eggs but some give birth to live young.

Scavenger An animal that feeds on animals that have died or been killed, or on dead plants and fungi.

Species A group of living things that share similar characteristics, such as shape, size, and coloring.

Spore A reproductive structure used by organisms because it can survive difficult conditions. Many bacteria, fungi, algae, and plants use spores.

Stomata (*Singular* stoma) Tiny openings in the outer layer of a leaf that allow gases in and out.

Thorax The area of an animal's body that lies between the head and the abdomen.

Vascular system A system of cells that carry water and nutrients around a plant.

Vertebrate An animal that has a backbone.

SCAVENGER

INDEX

Acknowledgments

Dorling Kindersley would like to thank the following for their kind permission to reproduce their photographs: (Key: a-above; b-below/bottom; c-center; f-far; l-left; r-right; t-top)

5 Dreamstime.com: Irochka (fbl). **Getty Images:** All Canada Photos / Tim Zurowski (fcla/hummingbird). **7 Science Photo Library:** Eye of Science (tl). **10 Science Photo Library:** Henning Dalhoff (fbl, bl, fclb); Paul Wootton (l). **11 SuperStock:** Robert Harding Picture Library (cr, fcr). **17 Corbis:** Photo Quest Ltd / Science Photo Library (br). **Science Photo Library:** Steve Gschmeissner (crb). **18 Fotolia:** Vadim Yerofeyev (cr). **Science Photo Library:** Eye Of Science (br); Dr. Kari Lounatmaa (fcr). **19 Science Photo Library:** National Cancer Institute (cr). **23 Dorling Kindersley:** Natural History Museum, London (tl). **24 Dreamstime.com:** Dannyphoto80 (cra); Andrey Sukhachev (cla); Irochka (ca). **25 Dreamstime.com:** Peter Wollinga (cla). **26 Dorling Kindersley:** Barry Hughes (crb); Natural History Museum, London (cl, c); Robert Royse (fcrb). **Getty Images:** Tim Laman / National Geographic (bl). **26–27 Dorling Kindersley:** Jon Hughes. **27 Jonathan Keeling:** (bl). **33 Dorling Kindersley:** Natural History Museum, London (bl). **Science Photo Library:** Steve Gschmeissner (bl). **35 Dreamstime.com:** Cosmin—Constantin Sava (clb). **37 Dorling Kindersley:** Jeremy Hunt—modelmaker (fbr). **38 Alamy Images:** Brand X Pictures (clb/beetle). **Dorling Kindersley:** Natural History Museum, London (cb/butterfly, crb/moth); Jerry Young (br/woodlouse). **39 Dorling Kindersley:** Natural History Museum, London (bl, fbr); Jerry Young (cl). **40 Corbis:** Bettmann (br). **41 Alamy Images:** Carolina Biological Supply Company / PhotoTake Inc. (bl); Dennis Kunkel Microscopy, Inc. / PhotoTake Inc. (cr); MicroScan / PhotoTake Inc. (br). **Corbis:** Mediscan (tc). **Getty Images:** Visuals Unlimited, Inc. / Kenneth Bart (tr); Visuals Unlimited / RMF (cra). **Science Photo Library:** Eye of Science (cla); Power and Syred (tl); Edward Kinsman (tl). **SuperStock:** Science Photo Library (crb). **42 Corbis:** Visuals Unlimited (clb). **Dorling Kindersley:** David Peart (cla). **Science Photo Library:** Dr. Kari Lounatmaa (cl). **SuperStock:** Robert Harding Picture Library (tr). **43 Corbis:** Jonathan Blair (clb). **SuperStock:** Robert Harding Picture Library (cl). **44 Alamy Images:** Paul Fleet (bl). **Dorling Kindersley:** Jamie Marshall (fcrb/parrot). **Getty Images:** Nick Koudis / Digital Vision (fclb/koala); Photodisc / Gail Shumway (fcrb/frog); David Tipling / Digital Vision (br). **45 Dreamstime.com:** Dreamzdesigner (br). **49 Dorling Kindersley:** Jamie Marshall (bl). **50 Dorling Kindersley:** David Peart (cl). **Getty Images:** Luis Marden / National Geographic (c). **SuperStock:** Science Faction (cr). **51 Corbis:** Lars-Olof Johansson / Naturbild (tr); Visuals Unlimited (cr). **53 Alamy Images:** Rick & Nora Bowers (clb/deer mouse). **Dreamstime.com:** Aspenphoto (cl/deer). **55 Science Photo Library:** Dr. Kari Lounatmaa (cb). **SuperStock:** imagebroker.net (br). **56 Corbis:** Philippe Crochet / Photononstop (fcl). **Getty Images:** Discovery Channel Images / Jeff Foott (bc). **NASA:** (cl). **58 Dorling Kindersley:** Newquay Zoo (tl). **58–59 Corbis:** John Lund (c). **Getty Images:** All Canada Photos / Tim Zurowski (ca). **59 Corbis:** DLILLC / Tim Davis (tl). **60 Dorling Kindersley:** Peter Minister—modelmaker (cl, bl/termites). **61 Getty Images:** Oxford Scientific / Mary Plage (cra); Oxford Scientific / David Fox (crb). **SuperStock:** Robert Harding Picture Library (cr). **68 Dorling Kindersley:** Gary Stabb—modelmaker (bl). **70 Alamy Images:** Nigel Pavitt /

John Warburton-Lee Photography (cr). **Dorling Kindersley:** Jerry Young (bc). **71 Alamy Images:** Michael Callan / FLPA (clb); Jeremy Pembrey (cr); Nicolas Chan (c). **Dorling Kindersley:** Natural History Museum, London (cl); Jerry Young (bc); Sean Hunter Photography (fbr). **72 Corbis:** Clouds Hill Imaging Ltd. (bl). **Getty Images:** Photographer's Choice / Kendall McMinimy (tl). **SuperStock:** Minden Pictures (tl). **73 Alamy Images:** David Fleetham (crb). **Corbis:** DLILLC / Tim Davis (cr). **Dorling Kindersley:** Natural History Museum, London (clb). **Getty Images:** Stone / Bob Elsdale (bl). **74 Dorling Kindersley:** Mike Read (cr); Gary Stabb—modelmaker (cl); Brian E. Small (c). **75 Dorling Kindersley:** Gary Stabb—modelmaker (cr). **Science Photo Library:** Courtesy of Crown Copyright Fera (cl). **76 Corbis:** Winfried Wisniewski (c). **Getty Images:** Gallo Images / Travel Ink (bl). **77 Corbis:** Ocean (bc). **Getty Images:** The Image Bank / Jeff Hunter (cl); Oxford Scientific / Chris Sharp (cra); Photographer's Choice / Nash Photos (cr). **78 Alamy Images:** Poelzer Wolfgang (br). **78–79 Dorling Kindersley:** Hunstanton Sea Life Centre, Hunstanton, Norfolk (c). **79 Dreamstime.com:** Olga Khoroshunova (crb); Rachwal (tl). **80–81 Corbis:** John Lund (bl/sky). **80 Corbis:** John Lund (bl/sky). **Getty Images:** All Canada Photos / Tim Zurowski (clb). **84 Dreamstime.com:** Kirill Zdorov (cl). **85 Getty Images:** AFP Photo / Hrvoje Polan (bl). **86 Science Photo Library:** Eye of Science (cla); Martin Oeggerli (cb); David McCarthy (crb). **87 Science Photo Library:** Thierry Berrod / Mona Lisa Production (cra); Eye of Science (cla); BSIP VEM (bl, cb); Steve Gschmeissner (crb). **88 Alamy Images:** Robert Pickett / Papilio (cr); Jeff Rotman (c). **Getty Images:** Panoramic Images (cl). **89 Alamy Images:** blickwinkel / Hartl (cl); Frans Lanting Studio (c). **90 Alamy Images:** blickwinkel / Patzner (cl). **Corbis:** Kevin Schafer (cr). **90–91 NASA: / NOAA. 91 Dorling Kindersley:** Jamie Marshall (br/sand); Natural History Museum, London (br/horseshoe crab). **92 Dorling Kindersley:** London Planetarium (tr). **93 NASA:** JPL (clb, crb); JPL-Caltech (fclb); USGS / Tammy Becker and Paul Geissler (fcrb). **94 Dorling Kindersley:** Natural History Museum, London (cl).

All other images © Dorling Kindersley

For further information see: www.dkimages.com